Advance praise for

CLASS DISMISSED

"Comic, cautionary, and delightfully bizarre . . . should be mandatory reading for student affairs staffs everywhere."

—ANDERS HENRIKSSON, author of the *New York Times* bestseller *Non Campus Mentis: World History According to College Students*

"*Class Dismissed* is unbelievably funny. It's like a hilarious night of stories with good college friends—except these friends publish your obituary while you're still alive." —PAUL DAVIDSON, author of *The Lost Blogs: From Jesus to Jim Morrison*

"These stories remind me of the wonderful idiots at my school. Actually, I think some are from those same idiots."

—STEVE HOFSTETTER, comedian and author of *Student Body Shots: A Sarcastic Look at the Best 4–6 Years of Your Life*

"The outrageous experiences in *Class Dismissed* will make you laugh out loud as well as wince when you recognize your own painfully embarrassing college memories." —CARRIE AIZLEY and CHRISTEN SUSSIN, the Oxygen Network's "Campus Ladies"

"Take my word for it as an expert on bathrooms: this book belongs in yours." —DAVE PRAEGER, editor, PoopReport.com

ALSO BY BEN APPLEBAUM
AND DERRICK PITTMAN

*Turd Ferguson & the Sausage Party:
An Uncensored Guide to College Slang*

CLASS
DISMISSED

Ben Applebaum,

Ryan McNally,

and Derrick Pittman

VILLARD Ⓥ NEW YORK

CLASS
DISMISSED

75 Outrageous, Mind-Expanding College Exploits

(and Lessons That Won't Be on the Final)

A Villard Books Trade Paperback Original

Copyright © 2006 by Ben Applebaum, Ryan McNally,
and Derrick Pittman

All rights reserved.

Published in the United States by Villard Books,
an imprint of The Random House Publishing Group, a division
of Random House, Inc., New York.

VILLARD and "V" CIRCLED Design are registered
trademarks of Random House, Inc.

ISBN 0-8129-7446-8

Printed in the United States of America

www.villard.com

2 4 6 8 9 7 5 3 1

Book design by Victoria Wong

CONTENTS

Introduction   xi

SECTION ONE
LIVING ARRANGEMENTS

Chapter 1. Room (Dis)Service   3
Studies in Nightmare Roommates

Epic Roommate Manifesto ▪ Feet Freak Roommate ▪ The Mars Rites

Chapter 2. Write Me Up, Scotty   11
Examining the Lost Art of RA-Student Relations

The Gag and the Jacket ▪ It Go Like This, I Don't Go Like That ▪ The Ultimate
RA Revenge

Chapter 3. House of Horrors   18
A Survey of Deplorable Living Conditions

A Little Batty ▪ Bumps in the Night ▪ Evil Pig ▪ House of the Sinking Feeling

SECTION TWO
RELATIONSHIPS

Chapter 4. What's Your Sign or Major?   31
Introduction to the Pickup

Knockout in a Thong ▪ Irish Accent Thwarted ▪ Faith Under Fire ▪ Don't
Drink the Punch

Chapter 5. Creeping Creeps 41

An Overview of Stalking Strategies

Trashing Tampa Psycho ▪ Grad Student Stalker ▪ For the Love and Stalking of Martin

Chapter 6. Screwing Up Screwing 49

Contemporary Studies in Unromantic Moments

The Odds Are Against Me ▪ Fiery Passion ▪ Do the Hustle

SECTION THREE
AUTHORITY

Chapter 7. The Parent Trap 59

Psychology of the Parent-Child Relationship

Horny and Hiding ▪ Parents Versus the Party ▪ Meet the Parents

Chapter 8. School Daze 101 67

Teachers, Cheating, and Other Academic Misadventures

Pardon, Frenchy? ▪ Professor Pain-in-the-Ass-and-Foot ▪ To Catch a Cheat ▪ Professorial Inspiration

Chapter 9. F——— the Police 77

Cops, College Students, and Other Legal Questions

The Not-So-Best Arrest ▪ The Nazi Cops ▪ Mugging for the Camera

Chapter 10. System of a Clown 86

A History of Revolution and Battling the Administration

Our Lady of Shameless Scams ▪ Community Full Service ▪ Mascot Madness ▪ Sisters in Charity Cheating

SECTION FOUR
DUMB SMARTIES

Chapter 11. And We Could've Gotten Away with It 101

Analysis of the Botched Scheme

The Chipper Stripper ▪ Hooters and Honors ▪ Caught Hot-Handed

Chapter 12. Lady Luck's Biatch 107

Criticism of Bad Bets, Stupid Dares

The Pepper and the Pecker ▪ The Power Twister ▪ Pizzalicious

Chapter 13. One Giant Step Back 115

A Survey of Just Dumb Moves

Weird Science ▪ The Pumpkin Bomb ▪ Rug and the Monkey Sheep

SECTION FIVE
THE PARTY

Chapter 14. Thinking Outside the Box of Wine 125

Advanced Party Techniques

Indoor Winter Beach Party ▪ Party Goes Up, Party Goes Down ▪ Magic Carpet Ride

Chapter 15. Beyond the Lamp Shade 132

A Review of Party Fouls and Social Missteps

Plenty of Party Fouls ▪ Fun on Pee Hill ▪ Getting Tanked with the Stars ▪ Falling for Claire Danes

Chapter 16. Dead to the World 140

Exploring the Inappropriate Pass-Out

Chicken Driven Wild ▪ Puff Puff Pass-Out ▪ Easter Resurrection ▪ From Wild Start to Finnish

Chapter 17. Poopers of the Party 148

A Survey of That Guy and That Girl

Epic Party Adventure ▪ The Pantyhose Nightmare ▪ Acid Trip ▪ That Girl Who Could Fly

SECTION SIX
TRAVEL

Chapter 18. The Stink from the Backseat 159

A Tribute to the Road Trip

The Munchies Mecca ▪ Midnight in Rosebud ▪ Floored and Floored

Chapter 19. Seven-Day Hedonists 166

An Anthology of Spring Breaks

Hanging with the Girls ■ Moms Gone Wild ■ Toppled and Topless

Chapter 20. International Procrastination 173

A Study in Studying Abroad

Greek Toga ■ Giovanni's Ego ■ The Swedish Attaché

SECTION SEVEN
THE AMAZING COLLEGE STUDENT

Chapter 21. Busting Balls and Exploding Ovens 183

In Defense of Classic Pranking and Revenge

Lou Can't Be Beet ■ Toasted in Bed ■ Aussie STD Scare Scam ■ Squeal
Like a Pig

Chapter 22. Premeditated Mayhem 191

Devious Applications of Genius

Harvard Proves It Sucks ■ The Few, the Proud, and the Ramen ■ Laying Cable
at the Russian House ■ Canty's Obituary Revenge

Final Thoughts 199
Acknowledgments 201

INTRODUCTION

I have never let my schooling
interfere with my education.
—Mark Twain

You don't have to go to college.
This isn't Russia. Is this Russia? This isn't Russia.
—Ty Webb (*Caddyshack*)

College: What's in It for Me?

How much would you pay for a piece of paper? Not just any piece of papyrus, but one with fancy fonts, Greek words, and the signatures of old men whom you've never met. Ten dollars? Fifty dollars? Try more than one hundred thousand dollars. And, to top it off, that piece of paper is as worthless on the market as those barely touched textbooks of yours. Feeling screwed yet?

But just because they call it a diploma, people will beg, compete, and go into years of debt for it. "All hail the mother-f'ing diploma!" the world tells us—in so many words.

Well, it didn't sound right to us, either. So it got us thinking: Besides said sheet of paper, what do you really get out of the four to eight years in the collegiate domain?

- *A better job?* Not necessarily. Just ask your waiter what Ivy League school he crewed for and you'll see that a degree alone doesn't a successful career make. Great leaders and pioneers such as Bill Gates, Madonna, and Ron Jeremy owe their success to drive, determination, and pure phallic fortitude. Not to degrees.
- *A smarter noodle?* Perhaps. But the academic pursuits described in university brochures are largely the stuff of a guidance counselor's wet

dreams, not of real life. Let's be honest. When in life has your fate ever hinged precariously on your

> **Fenchel duality theorem:**
> $f^*(y) = \sup\{\langle x,y\rangle - f(x)\}$

knowing the Fenchel duality theorem? And if it has, could the hungover TA they passed off as your instructor have helped you with it?

■ *A network of contacts?* Sort of. Alumni whom you've never met are as likely to help you as, say, someone who shares the same dry cleaner with you. But the college friends you drank with, ran from the cops with, and stole cable from exchange students with—those are the ones who'll have your back for years to come.

The Big Stinkin' Deal About College

So why go through—and, more important, why pay for—a higher education? First off, college is about new experiences. It's a crucial time, a time to tap into new ideas, new adventures, and new icy cold kegs. It's a time when it's acceptable to steal toilet paper yet spend your life savings on a decorative glass bong. And since this behavior isn't tolerated in the real world, college is an ideological playground worth hopping the fence for.

College is also hypersocial. We can't speak intelligently about the importance of college bonding in the face of the weakening social capital in our communities. Too bad. But we do know that unless you're in the military or you play for a ragtag team of American hockey underdogs, you'll never make friends like the ones you make in college.

Finally, college is a time of transition. Since we no longer have to earn our adulthood by living off squirrel meat in the woods for three months, college provides this initiation. The transition from naive and wide-eyed teenager to wise and unemployed adult helps develop something new in us: maturity. Sure, you may not feel mature at that Cancún foam party, but rest assured, the seeds of maturity have been planted—and thoroughly watered with Red Bull.

So all of these factors get stirred together like a cheap grain punch to create a truly unique experience. Ironically, most of the time at college you don't even know how good you have it. But every now and then, you wake up, turn to the coyote-ugly hookup or stolen yard gnome next to you in bed, and realize that this is truly an extraordinary time—and worth the lifetime of debt.

And from this four-year, all-you-can-eat buffet of life, your college stories are the doggie bags—tidy little tidbits from the grand spread. But unlike real doggie bags, they don't get thrown out after a month. No, these stories get reheated and shared for years and years to come.

It is our unsupportable—and admittedly quite suspect—theory that amazing college experiences are what teach you the most valuable lessons you can learn in life. Ones not covered on any exams or even in those professor-authored textbooks.

Can shaming a passed-out roommate teach creativity? Can stalking teach persistence? Can a golden shower teach the golden rule? We'll get back to you on that last one. But we do know that twenty years later, you'll still be talking about it.

Who Died and Made Us Experts?

We should know what makes a great college story. We've become downright connoisseurs of the subject. After a few years in the cubicled post-collegiate life, we began to notice that conversations with friends, co-workers, and neighbors invariably turned to a recounting of college tales. It seemed that the more the real world constricted, the more people liked to relive their heady days on campus.

This truth inspired CollegeStories.com, our little nook on the Net. On our site, it is always the Sunday after a wild weekend, and time for people to share their most memorable exploits and adventures. After running this site for all these years, we've read thousands of real stories from campuses around the world—from universities large and small, public and private, and world renowned and obscure (Erskin College, where you at?).

We've read them all. And we've gained a critical eye for the finest stories (and strong stomachs to deal with the rest). For a story to make the cut for this book, two key criteria had to be met:

CollegeStories.com launched on June 10, 1999, with just three stories. Today it has more than three thousand.

1. They gots to be entertaining. This criterion should actually be the only rule. One through five. What's the point of reading cloying college success stories? (Sorry to all *Chicken Soup for the College Soul* readers.) But since amusement is subjective, we offer a food court's worth of variety. A little fetish partying and apartment flooding here. A little Ivy League pranks and cult leader roommates there. Who needs another book of intellectual wealth and substance? The world needs a book that can be read on the can. And this is it.
2. They must be unique. These stories distinguish themselves from the mass of "Yo, I got shit-faced last night" tales. Some pack a surprising twist ("Hooters and Honors," page 103); others play out in fiery epistolary exchanges ("Epic Roommate Manifesto," page 4), but all stand out from the three thousand we've catalogued.

So you're asking yourself: Are these stories true? First, we prefer the term "true-ish." We've tried to sift through the B.S. and find well-told stories that our authors stand by. Second, this book is shelved in the Humor section, not the Verified Facts for Nerds section. So please, just read rule number one and enjoy.

Appreciating the Debaucherous Arts

Why combine the best college stories into a book? Much like assembling great art into a museum, we hope to encourage appreciation of these works in this compendium. And like great works of art, the best college stories can be grouped together based on common themes. Instead of abstract expressionism, Pop Art, and surrealism, though, we're talking "Devious Applications of Genius," "Studies in Unromantic Moments," and "A Survey of Deplorable Living Conditions." As you read through these and other chapters, we hope that you will gain an appreciation for the subtle allusions, emotional subtext, and expert use of the f-bomb that come to light when the best college stories are examined together. If you're lucky, you might see yourself in some of these stories. If you're unlucky, you might literally recognize yourself as a character in one of these stories.

Either way, we hope that this book will help you take a new look at the college experience, seeing the memories as the real prizes of graduation and the diploma as merely a fancy, expensive framed receipt.

P.S. If you've read this entire introduction, then you deserve a big, sloppy kiss. But since that's creepy, we're giving out free goodies instead. Go to CollegeStories.com/goodies, and get yours while supplies last.

LIVING ARRANGEMENTS

Tell me whom you live with,
and I will tell you who you are.
—Spanish proverb

In theory, the college dorm should be a relatively tranquil haven where one studies, sleeps, and enjoys the occasional snack. Yet the reality is often as ugly as the slice of pizza that's been in your mini-fridge for three months.

Thrust into a cramped living area, the college student must cope with a roommate who doesn't share his views on politics, music, or hygiene; an RA whose primary goal is making the collegiate experience miserable; and the squalor of two semesters without a drop of Mr. Clean.

Forget the classroom; the college dorm is where the true preparation for the real world begins. If you can put up with an obnoxious roommate for a year, then interacting with the weirdo in the cubicle next to yours, who bears a distinct resemblance to Milton in *Office Space,* will be a cakewalk. Learn to make peace with the RA—or better yet, antagonize him and get away with it—and you're set for dealing with your tight-ass boss. And of course, finding out that neglecting your cleaning duties can lead to armadillos overrunning your off-campus house is great preparation for becoming a homeowner.

The following chapters show that although dropping one hundred thousand dollars over four years doesn't necessarily guarantee a pleasant living experience, it does make for some sweetness in the storytelling department.

CHAPTER 1

Room (Dis)Service

Studies in Nightmare Roommates

The Odd Couple, the classic film comedy starring Jack Lemmon and Walter Matthau, is the hilarious tale of two completely mismatched roommates. In college campuses across the globe, this humorous scenario plays out on a daily basis—but without the wacky TV spin-off.

Navigating around the idiosyncrasies of your roommate can be part of the fun of college life. But sometimes you stumble across a roommate whose behavior leans toward the extreme—a cult meeting here, an acute case of floorphobia there. These incidents may seem like a good reason to get the hell out of Dodge and give homeschooling a try. But the communication and negotiation skills you learn in the process of dealing with these "unique" characters will pay dividends, as will the patience you'll develop along the way. And Dodge starts looking a whole lot better.

They say that those who live in glass houses shouldn't throw stones. But if the words, actions, and black candle wax tossed around in these stories are any indication, it's safe to say that college dorms are made from the thickest of cement.

Epic Roommate Manifesto

Before my senior year began, one of our new roommates (whom I had not yet met) decided to e-mail the other boys in the group his requirements if we were to "live together peacefully." Following his little manifesto is my reply.

The Manifesto

Dear future roommates,

   A lot of these things are simply common courtesy—things that should never come up and probably won't. This list is by no means comprehensive, but is everything I could think of.

1. **Keep the door locked.** If you're the last person to leave the room, lock the door. Yes, this means that you will have to carry a key on you every time you go out.

> Before coauthoring *The Communist Manifesto,* Karl Marx enjoyed the sauce in college as a leader of the Trier Tavern Club.

2. **Keep quiet.** It's hard for me to sleep while a conversation is going on. Noise by itself and light don't bother me as much. For example, my roommate Garret last year could stay up with a desk lamp reading and typing on his computer with the volume turned down, and I was fine.

3. **No alcohol.** That means no drinking alcohol in the room and no keeping alcohol in the room. If you plan on drinking, go somewhere else. This is a dry campus, and I'll have no qualms about calling the RA on you or the cops if you're underage.

4. **No sex in the room.** Rent a room in a hotel or go to her room. This is just common respect.

5. **No pot, no illicit drugs, etc.** You get my drift. I'll call the cops before I call campus security.

6. **Message-taking is sacrosanct.** If you forget a message, that's okay. Not answering the phone and letting it go to voice mail is also fine. I'm not talking about unintentional stuff, but if you intentionally decide not to relay a message, or make up messages as part of some sort of joke, I assure you that I won't take it as a joke.

7. **No cohabiting.** As far as I'm concerned, if female friends are over really late and fall asleep while watching a movie, then it's okay to let them

spend the night. This is not a license for having your girlfriend live in the room, nor should sleeping over be a common event. If it's planned (e.g., you have a female friend coming for a visit), I would like to know beforehand.

8. **No smoking.** If you need to smoke, go outside. If you go to a smoke-filled bar, I'd appreciate it if you changed after you got home and took your clothes somewhere to air out, so that the room won't get filled with smoke.

9. **No porn (that I can see).** No mags in the bathroom that aren't hidden away in your own little drawer. No porno posters in the living room, bathroom, or in your room that I can see from the living room. This includes porn screen savers. If you wish to watch a porn video, I'd appreciate it if you did it somewhere else.

10. **Hands off my computer.** This isn't a "don't mess" rule. This is: do not touch without permission. If, after getting to know you, I find that you are worthy of my trust, this rule might change to some extent. But for now, don't touch.

I hope I haven't come off as a busybody rules lawyer. I just think that it is beneficial to have all this stuff out in the open as early as possible. I really do look forward to when we move in.

Now a little about me. I am a born-again Christian. I go to church most every Sunday and sometimes on other days as well. Politically, I am conservative. I have no party affiliation, but if I had to choose between Democrats and Republicans, I would choose Republicans in an instant. I am a senior majoring in Computer Science (focus on Java programming) with a minor in Math. My favorite TV show is *Babylon 5*. In general, I like fantasy, sci-fi, and computer stuff. Anthony suggested that we discuss our rooming arrangements before we arrived at school, which I think is an excellent idea. Toward that end, I have provided my thoughts on the matter: First things first, I won't room with Luke. This is based on what I know of him personally and the testimonies of other people who know him. My personal

> **THE DORKINESS SLANG SCALE**
>
> **Packing Peanut**—An annoying hanger-on.
> **Tool**—Similar to a nerd, but not as smart.
> **Wedge**—The simplest tool—even more insulting.
> **Zero**—A person with nothing to offer.

preference for roommates will be based on prayer, what people tell me about themselves, and any additional information that I may gather. I'll let everyone know, at the same time, what I think.

—*James*

The Reply

Hello, James.

My name is Luke Vukovich, I'm sure you've heard of me and read about me in the newspaper, or perhaps you've seen me on TV.

For the full uncensored response, visit CollegeStories.com/manifesto.

In any case, I'm really looking forward to getting to know you. Although I may not fit into the "Christian" mentality you espouse, I have always believed myself to be a person of character and integrity. I'm respectful of other people's beliefs and preferences.

I'm pleased that you have formulated a rather extensive list of what you require so that your God-fearing lifestyle will not be interrupted. However, you have broken my one, BIG, all-encompassing rule:

1. **Too many rules.**

That's about it. Additionally, I thoroughly desire to go to Hell. You see, James, I am one of those people who think that if you're not hurting someone else, you should be able to do whatever you like. Forgive my heathenistic ignorance, but I fail to see how fucking my own girlfriend, in my own room, should be any of your business—or that of any RA, for that matter.

I would have been more than willing to accommodate your views and been tolerant of them. We could have even been friends. All you would have had to do is tolerate my freedom. Your laundry list of requirements leads me to believe that you are very intolerant of other people's lifestyles, and I find this very insulting. Furthermore, any male who would conform to your rules and live in fear of them needs to have his testicles re-attached.

If I'm fortunate enough to live with you, and you decide to enforce any one of the rules contained in your little manifesto, I look forward to thoroughly violating your computer. I have a collection of about ten disks loaded with the latest viruses, and I have been waiting a long time to find a holy-rolling, boner-biting, fuck face like you upon whom I could unleash them.

If any of these statements offends you, perhaps you should find another room. Have fun next year,
—*Luke*

—*California Lutheran University*

Alumni Update: "On move-in day, James was frantically running around trying to find another room that would suit his fundamentalist sensitivities. He failed and ended up staying with us. Things simmered down, but we didn't speak much for the rest of the year."

LESSON LEARNED: Difficult, opinionated people are best fought with difficult, opinionated rhetoric. If you are one of the few, the proud, the intelligent, then be sure to apply your smarts to a good cause: putting a self-righteous tool in his place.

Feet Freak Roommate

My roommate and I don't get along too well. To put it gently, let's just say she doesn't have the "social skills" to deal with people. And she has one small quirk—well, actually, a big one. See, she refuses to touch the clean, carpeted floor with anything less than sandals on her feet, not even with socks. She always has her sandals at the base of the ladder so that when she gets down from her bunk, she can avoid contact with the floor for even a moment.

> The fear of touching or being touched is called aphephobia.

So, a month or two ago she went to the Meijer supercenter with a few girls. On that trip, she was busted trying to steal two CDs. For some reason, she didn't go to jail. She was merely sent home with a fine and a court date. She failed to show for her court date, which resulted in a warrant being issued for her arrest.

The day came when the cops banged on our dorm door. Unfortunately, I wasn't around until about three hours later, but when I arrived, everyone on my floor was eager to fill me in on the cops' appearance.

Everyone, including the cops, suspected that my roommate was in the room refusing to come to the door. When I arrived, the door was locked, and all the lights were off. It "appeared" that she was gone, but my keen eye noticed that every pair of shoes she owned, even the sandals, were in their shoe area. So I knew she had to be somewhere in the eight-by-ten room. But I didn't look. I suspected she was hiding in her wardrobe, and I thought it would be much funnier if the cops found her there instead of me.

My RA called the cops to inform them that I was back in the building, and I told them I would give them permission to come into the room. The county sheriff arrived, followed by three campus police, and they entered my room and crowded around the wardrobe. Sadly, after talking to her, coaxing her to come out, they finally opened the wardrobe door, finding nothing but clothes and a jacket.

I wasn't sure what to say, because I had been certain she was in the room. But the sheriff wasn't giving up and decided to search behind the bunk beds and dressers. And there he found her hiding. But even after he acknowledged seeing her, she still wouldn't budge. He was yelling at her the whole time, but it wasn't until he began to dismantle the bunk beds that she finally came out.

Now, to the best part of the story: As she was being handcuffed, I observed her feet. To my amazement, she was standing on her heels because she was only in her socks. Do you really think that while being arrested you'd be concerned with your feet touching the carpet?

On the bright side, I'm working on getting my own room for the remainder of the semester, due to the "traumatic experience" I've endured.

—Grand Valley State University

> Eccentric billionaire aviator Howard Hughes wore tissue boxes on his feet to protect them from germs. No word what his roommate said about that.

LESSON LEARNED: This author gets it. You need to look for, then exploit the proverbial silver lining in every situation. Ask for upgrades, lobby for free drinks, get the single room—work the system for your own benefit. If not, you're leaving money on the table. That is, unless your psycho roommate hasn't already stolen the money off said table.

The Mars Rites

Going into my sophomore year, I was paired with a transfer-student roommate. I'm not one to pass judgment on anybody, but I did feel a bit uncomfortable when the guy came in wearing black lipstick and black eye shadow.

He was the palest person I'd ever seen and had long black hair. He introduced himself as "Mars," although I later saw his real name, Kevin Michaels, on a tuition statement he left out in the open. The first month or so went fine, as we both basically kept to ourselves. Soon, four other "Mars look-alikes" were visiting the room on a daily basis, and strange things began to happen.

I would return to the dorms late at night and find black candle wax all over the floor. On one occasion, I re-

> The month of March is named after Mars, the Roman god of war.

turned to find that Mars had changed our bulb from normal to black. I changed the bulb back, and to my surprise, this totally enraged him. He accused me of interfering with the "Mars rites." I didn't know what the hell he was talking about, but I soon found out.

Just a couple of nights later, I awoke at 2:00 A.M. to find that a black sheet was hanging from the ceiling, dividing his side of the room from mine. Glowing candlelight was coming from his side. I asked him what was going on, only to find him in a meditating position with his eyes rolled back in his head. He was wearing some sort of black cloak. I asked him again what was up, and his response was, "I, Lord Mars, am getting stronger, and you are forbidden to enter my side."

To make matters worse, his Mars look-alikes began to join him during these weekly rituals. Remarkably, I made it through the year, and at long last, the final weekend we were to be roommates rolled around. My girlfriend, Porsche, my best friend, George, and George's girlfriend, Kirsten, were making the trip from

> Frank Mars and his son Forrest created such classic candies as M&M's, Milky Way, and Snickers.

Ohio to visit me. I asked Mars to please not pull his bullshit this weekend, as I had company coming in.

He told me that nothing interfered with the Mars rites. I responded that if he pulled any shit, I would kick his Marsite ass. He then told me that the Marsites fear nobody. I warned him again, and then left to meet up with my friends. At around midnight, they requested to see my dorm. I was hesitant, but gave in.

When we arrived, I found Mars and his look-alikes having one of their rituals. They were sitting in meditating positions with their eyes rolled back in their heads. The black sheet was down, and some of them were sitting on *my bed*. Black candle wax had been poured all over the floor, and even on my sheets. At least ten candles were burning, and the black bulb was on.

Porsche, George, and Kirsten looked on in horror. I shouted at the Mars look-alikes to get the hell out. Mars looked at me, rolled his eyes back in his head again, and in his best demonic voice said, "Our prey has arrived." That's when I lost it and punched him square in the nose. He fell back and knocked a burning candle onto his bed. The sheets were engulfed in flames, but his cult followers put the fire out with their drinks, some sort of red substance, probably Kool-Aid. Then they all turned toward me.

I reached around my dresser and pulled out my aluminum baseball bat. I told them all to "get out before I start swinging!" They left, one of them helping Mars walk as he tended to his bloody nose. I was so upset that my friends and I left and stayed in a hotel for the weekend. I returned to the dorm Sunday evening expecting some heat from the college administration. To my surprise, Mars was nowhere in sight, and all his property was gone from the room. I found out the next day that he had dropped out and moved back home. Not a word about my punching him was mentioned to the administration. Since that bizarre incident, I've seen his fellow Marsites from time to time walking around campus. Not surprisingly, they've shed their dark image.

I'm the first to admit that I hate violence, but that was one punch worth throwing. My thoughts and prayers go out to anyone who has to put up with that guy.

—*University of Louisville*

LESSON LEARNED: Despite what you may think after watching too much E!, posses and entourages aren't reserved for the famous, the popular, or even the sane. When someone rolls up like they're the shit, just remember that even a weenie in college can lead a cult, so it doesn't take much.

CHAPTER 2

Write Me Up, Scotty

Examining the Lost Art of RA-Student Relations

They're your age, but they have the power to break you. They're normal-looking people with a seemingly supernatural ability to hear every conversation on the hall, not to mention to sniff out beer and other illicit substances stashed in your room. They are the dreaded resident advisors.

How they went from fun-loving frosh to upperclassmen out to ruin the good times of their peers is a mystery. The reasons may continue to elude us, but one truth remains: with rare exception, RAs simply suck.

But they do play a crucial role in the collegiate experience—providing a ready foil to the college students they watch over and bearing witness to those students' foolish, bizarre, and often idiosyncratic shenanigans (like real-life Mr. Ropers or Furleys). And occasionally, as you'll read, they even get some pretty sweet revenge.

Other than providing good entertainment, is there any point to this classic rivalry? You betcha. Learning to live under the reign of a dictator—and figuring out when and how to get in a well-timed dig—comes in mighty handy when dealing with the autocratic bosses you'll inevitably cross paths with in the working world.

As the college experience continues to evolve, it's safe to say that the conflict between students and RAs will remain an amusing constant.

The Gag and the Jacket

This unfortunate incident happened during my freshman year. I lived in a dorm and roomed with one of those "Goth" chicks. She liked to go out to raves and Goth clubs and had lots of fetish stuff.

Among the many accessories in her all-black wardrobe were a black leather straitjacket and a ball gag. She wore the straitjacket with the arms undone a couple of times to her raves, but I think the ball gag was just something novel she had. She kept it on her dresser, strapped around this Styrofoam head that had

a pink wig on it. A little bizarre, sure, but I could live with it. Anyway, I asked her about the straitjacket one time, and she asked if I wanted to try it on.

It was late and past quiet hours, so I figured, what the heck. I was curious about what it was like and if I could get out of it. So she strapped me up in it. A few minutes later she asked if I wanted to try the gag, too. I was pretty uncomfortable with the idea, since I couldn't move my arms. I was really scared I would choke or something. She promised me she wouldn't keep it on me for very long.

Reluctantly, I opened my mouth, and she strapped the gag on. It was a pretty claustrophobic feeling, and I couldn't say a word or move. I struggled for a minute or two, and then suddenly we heard a knock at the door. My eyes went wide. I was going to die of embarrassment if anyone saw me strapped up in this straitjacket with a ball gag strapped in my mouth. This wasn't going to be exactly the easiest thing to explain. I could only imagine the stories that would get out. As bad as things were, they quickly got worse. Suddenly we heard, "RA on call. Open up." We couldn't stall. My roomie opened the door a crack and poked her head out. Naturally, the RA thought we

In his 1910 book *Handcuff Escapes*, Harry Houdini describes his technique for escaping from straitjackets—the keys are technical know-how and brute physical strength.

were hiding something and suspected we had alcohol or something in the room, so she pushed the door open. Of course, there I was all tied up, and I couldn't say anything.

For perhaps the first time in collegiate history, I had rendered an RA speechless. My roommate, in a desperate attempt to save face, quickly explained that I was just trying it on. As it turned out, the TV was up too loud, and that was what the knock had been about. We both got written up.

One little problem: I was tied up and therefore couldn't sign the warning, so the RA said she'd come back. She knew I was sort of embarrassed (to say the least), so she wrote the violation up quickly and then left. As soon as the door was closed, my roomie undid the ball gag and unbuckled the straitjacket. I signed the damn slip, and my roomie went down the hall and handed it to the RA.

That was the last time I ever experimented with anything like that. Fortunately, my foray into S&M stayed between the three of us.

—*University of North Texas*

LESSON LEARNED: Always remember: the freakier the shit you dabble in, the more likely it is that someone will walk in on you doing it. Don't believe us? Try getting intimate with a construction cone and a garden hose, then call us when you're busted by a permanently scarred loved one.

It Go Like This, I Don't Go Like That

I awoke after a raging night of partying and walked slowly back to the fraternity house. The outside world was gray and damp, reflecting the inner haze through which I also traveled. After fumbling with the door lock, I passed slowly inside into the foyer.

The stench of stagnant beer almost overwhelmed me. Furniture and liquor bottles lay strewn across the tile. Unknown fluids flowed together to form black, noisome pools in the wreckage. The dance floor was in the same state of disarray as the foyer, but the bits of bow and wrapping paper reminded me that this was the result of a Christmas party. Pious in name only, the party had degenerated into the most violent liquor party in recent history.

A faint light glowed in the far left corner of our chapter room. Under the lamp was an unstirring figure. It was lying on its back upon three couch cushions. It was unclad, save for a white T-shirt, white boxers, and one sock on its right foot. Its arm was thrown across its brow in a futile attempt to shield its eyes. Blond hair sprang back wildly.

"Wenis!" I shook him gently. "Wenis, are you okay?"

Out of some recessive alcoholic hibernation he came forth. His eyes opened to slits as he rose on one arm and uttered plaintively, "Help."

This was the first story on CollegeStories.com and a typical night for our friend Wenis. Since posting this story, we've learned that most people know a Wenis, too.

"Wenis, you're wearing one sock. What happened?"

"I don't know." His head flailed left to right, eyes shut tight. "I think I got written up by the RA. Help me, please. Help me find my pants."

"Where were you when you last had them?" I questioned.

"I don't know," he gasped. By this time, I was giggling maniacally.

I tramped through the house in a delighted mood looking for Wenis's phantom pants. But the pants were nowhere to be found. I was filled with glee. Where could they be?

I decided to go through the back door to check the stairwell we shared with independent student housing. Around one railing and up the first floor I flew. At the top of the second flight were the pants of the aforementioned Wenis. Filthy they were, with dark streaks marking the khaki legs. Doubled over in laughter, I reached to pick them up and found them inordinately heavy. At first I thought it to be the belt, but I investigated further. As my eyes moved up from cuff to waist, I made a remarkable discovery. The insoles of Wenis's shoes were stuffed into his pants pockets. I was dazed with awe and wonderment. What divine/alcoholic urging had caused him to render such a unique and ingenious gesture?

I fished further into his left pocket and found a folded piece of yellow carbon paper. I opened it cautiously. The sheet was a one-page synopsis of Wenis's struggle with an RA—and several inner demons:

The ancient Egyptian pharaoh Unas, the last king of the Fifth Dynasty, also went by the name Wenis. He, however, did not have to worry about RAs in the halls of the pyramid.

Resident Violation Report

It was approximately 3 A.M., December 9, when we responded to the sound of loud crashing coming from the third floor. I ran up the fraternity stairwell and met the other RA on duty. On our arrival, we found a student throwing trash cans off the third-floor balcony.

We questioned him, but his words were so incoherent and his speech so slurred we could not understand what he was saying. When asked to produce his ID, he stated, "It go like this, but I don't go like that, swear to Christ." (We have absolutely no idea what this means.)

After we talked to him for a while, he handed us both his school and state IDs. He became unable to stand and leaned against the wall. There he began to fall asleep and hit his head, saying, "That hurt, swear to Christ."

We gave him a citation for public drunkenness and disorderly conduct and told him to go back to his room. We discussed this matter further, and we both feel he should undergo counseling and an evaluation.

—*Wake Forest University*

Alumni Update: Wenis is currently in law enforcement and has served in the war in Iraq. The irony that he is now the face of authority is not lost on us. Neither is the fear.

LESSON LEARNED: When you're up against authority figures in life, you can outthink them and know you can ultimately win. Or you can out-crazy them and wake up not knowing if you've won or where your pants are.

The Ultimate RA Revenge

I was nearing the end of my junior year and my last term as a residence director. Having followed some bad advice, I had accidentally hired two complete tool bags as my resident assistants. All of my residents loved tormenting these two RAs, "Redneck the Wonder RA" and "Saddle Bags Shelly." But there were two roommates in particular who thought that picking on a couple of RAs made them manlier. And they figured that if they could push the rest of the staff around, they could easily manipulate their RD as well.

Big mistake.

The guys started out trying to win me over by hitting on me. Unfortunately for them, I had figured out long ago that most of my residents just wanted to sleep with me for the fame of bagging their RD. After months of failed attempts to woo me, the boys began to try other tactics. They started pounding on my bedroom wall with hammers and bouncing basketballs against my windows. They would throw huge parties specifically on the nights I was on duty. When I would write them up, their trailer-trash girlfriends would scrawl all kinds of pleasant messages on my door. Being the slime that they were, they managed to weasel out of any real trouble each time.

I bided my time, however, knowing that good things come to those who wait. Especially revenge.

It was the last night of my term as RD, and I just happened to have my patio door open when I noticed my favorite residents walking in with their brand-new entertainment system. Feigning interest in their state-of-the-art system, I hung around and watched as they set up their new toy—on the floor of their apartment, directly in front of the door. That's when I got my idea.

I waited until about 3:00 A.M., and then I called one of my best buds and made her sneak into my building. She was bewildered by her unexpected wake-up call but caught on quickly when she saw me filling a fifty-five-gallon trash can with water. Taking a page out of Pennsylvania history, I decided that the conditions were right to re-create the infamous Johnstown Flood.

I used my master keys to lock every door in the hallway, ensuring that the coast would be clear. Then my friend and I dragged the very heavy can over to the two guys' apartment and positioned it against their door. Then I went to my room and prepared for act two. My bud drove to a nearby gas station, where she called

> In 1889, the city of Johnstown, Pennsylvania, was destroyed after the Lake Conemaugh dam broke.

my bad boys, pretending she was one of their random booty calls and was "locked out in the cold." Thinking a hookup was on the horizon, the boys didn't think twice and ran to the door. When they opened it, they upset the trash can, and fifty-five gallons of water flooded their apartment—completely frying their brand-new (and uninsured) entertainment system.

The boys ran to my apartment and woke me from my "slumber." Doe-eyed with innocence, I called campus police for them and helped them fill out a police report. Afterward, I went to sleep with a triumphant smile on my face.

—*University of Pittsburgh*

LESSON LEARNED: In times like these, you learn about reciprocity and the importance of not trying to take the high road when you're dealing with assholes who cruise the low. Get down, get dirty, get even.

CHAPTER 3

House of Horrors

A Survey of Deplorable Living Conditions

In an attempt to free themselves from the constraints of dorm life, some students opt to live in student apartments or off-campus housing. These new digs initially seem like paradise, with better roommates and less pestering from "the man." But like anything that seems too good to be true, it is.

You see, these living conditions bring new challenges. Separated from the safety net of Mommy and Daddy, and removed from the monitoring of RAs and janitors, a predictable squalor results. And yet, college students show a remarkable capacity for being unfazed as their homes crumble around them. That is, until a phalanx of insects, rodents, farm animals, or homeless squatters snaps them back into reality.

Lessons learned: (1) Attend to strange noises, smells, and sights immediately; (2) Don't room with anyone majoring in Entomology; and (3) Animals are smarter than the average college student.

But seriously, learning about the wonders of house upkeep will go a long way when you become a homeowner, especially if you're living with a spouse who's a little less forgiving than your college roomies.

In the meantime, sink your teeth into these tales. Just make sure there aren't any critters lurking under the couch you're sitting on.

A Little Batty

One day, I noticed there were squirrels in the attic of our off-campus house. I saw them going in and out of a hole near my chimney. After many late nights of waking up to squirrels scratching around in the attic, I decided to get the hole fixed. When the project was completed, my roommate and I climbed down the rope ladder, leaving it down so we could go back up and check on things. Later, I heard my dog going fucking nuts.

Somehow, my little Jack Russell terrier had climbed up the ladder and was furiously attacking the fiberglass insulation. When I went up to retrieve him, I heard some clicking and squeaking noises, which I assumed were baby squirrels. I told my friends what had happened, and we decided to look for the babies in the morning.

That morning, my roommate and I headed upstairs and noticed something odd: a little face peering out from inside the broken shutter of the attic ceiling fan. I couldn't tell what it was, but then it dropped out of the attic fan, hit the floor, got up, and started *flying around my house.*

Suddenly, it hit me like a Bruce Wayne punch to the gut: these were bats, not squirrels. I looked up and saw three more little faces in the opening. And then, within seconds, the bats were boiling out of my attic in a plague of biblical proportions.

We headed down the hall toward the stairs. I was in front, but I stopped because something in my room caught my eye. But before I could say anything, one of my friends let out the obligatory *Fear and Loathing* quote: "We can't stop here. This is bat country."

The common brown bat of North America is the world's longest-living mammal for its size, with a life span sometimes exceeding thirty-two years.

After we'd finished cracking up, I pointed out with considerably less humor that there were about twenty bats flying around in circles in my room. So, we quickly put on our "bat gear," which consisted of ski or paintball masks, long-sleeve shirts, and plastic rain ponchos, and grabbed brooms, badminton rackets, and Ping-Pong paddles. Properly attired, we charged back upstairs, which was now teeming with bats. We went from room to room clearing the bats, catching and releasing one bat at a time.

Fortunately, I'm not afraid of bats. In fact, I used to have one as a pet. However, my brother and my friend Shadow were huge sissies. Whenever a bat passed near either of them, it would send them screaming out of the room. Shadow filmed this whole ordeal, so every time a bat came near the camera there was a great *Blair Witch*–like effect of the cameraman turning around and running screaming in the opposite direction.

It took most of the night, but we removed almost every damn bat from my house, and aside from the ones my dog killed, all the bats survived to go off and live in some other person's attic.

> Tequila is produced from agave plants, whose seed production drops to one-three thousandth of normal without bat pollinators.

My advice? Next time you hear animal noises coming from the attic, deal with them sooner rather than later.

—*University of South Florida*

LESSON LEARNED: Be action-oriented, especially in a crisis. In life you can't sit back and let things happen. No, you need to stand up, put on your homemade armor, and swing at the challenges or bats you must face.

Bumps in the Night

This past weekend my roommates, Seth and Val, were relaxing in our house playing EverQuest, when they suddenly started hearing loud noises coming from our attic. A bit freaked out, they called me to see if I was messing with them. I assured them that I was at Rhonda's house drinking with some friends. Being the cool-headed gents they are, they then concluded that there was a ghost or some big-ass animals in our attic. I was mildly annoyed at being interrupted in my boozing to tend to their foolish paranoia, but I told them I'd come home and check it out.

As I was walking home, and becoming increasingly pissed that these guys were such wimps that they couldn't check out these noises themselves, I saw both my roommates in a fight with three random dudes. Holy crap! Not even thinking about the potential ramifications, I ran up and just blasted this one guy right in his grill. He dropped to the ground, where I began to kick him straight in his junk. Needless to say, it was an all-out melee.

When we finally had the situation under control, we let the three guys run off, beaten and bloodied. I turned to my friends and asked what the hell had happened. They told me that they kept hearing all these noises coming from upstairs, so they finally decided to check it out themselves. With increasing trepidation, they opened the attic door and discovered a most unexpected sight: three bums living in our attic. When my roommates confronted them and asked what they were doing there, all hell broke loose.

> The Brooklyn Dodgers became affectionately known as "Dem Bums" after suffering through a string of losing seasons during the Depression.

Apparently, they had gotten into the house before we moved in and had been living there the whole time. I told Val and Seth that that was probably why our food and money kept turning up missing. We all had a good laugh and went up to the attic to check out the bums' living quarters.

They had a good little setup. A bucket for relieving themselves. A cooler containing water and beer. Our missing bottle of Aftershock. A ton of our packaged food.

> The eighty-proof Aftershock comes in three main flavors: the blue "Cool Citrus" (mint), red "Hot & Cool" (cinnamon), and green "Thermal Bite" (spicy).

We cleaned it all up and then took out our trash. That's when the cops pulled up and said that we were under arrest for assaulting three men. Come again?

We went nuts. Seth and Val told the police what had happened and that we had proof. We showed them the little setup. Fortunately, the cops told us they believed our story and knew these dudes were bums, so they ended up hauling these guys away. Crisis averted.

Relieved, we all went back inside. Seth and Val went back to playing their game, and Rhonda came over with two of her friends. We all started drinking and reliving the unbelievable events that had occurred earlier. Needless to say, we stayed downstairs.

—*Syracuse University*

LESSON LEARNED: Trust your intuition. If something doesn't feel right, if you're not quite sure what's going bump in the night, then go with your gut. Our research shows that nine out of ten times it means you have a bad case of the bums.

Evil Pig

Brigham Young University is a pretty uptight school, and nearly everyone there is a practicing Mormon. Luckily, while I was a student there, we managed to have some wacky times nonetheless.

I decided to live with some of my cousins off campus. One of them worked at a pet store, so we always had way too many animals around. He was the type who liked to collect boa constrictors and tarantulas.

We ended up with a twenty-one-foot ball python in our kitchen, in an enormous Plexiglas-and-wood cage. The zoo didn't stop there. We also had an enormous Great Dane and an indoor tree full of flying squirrels. While it was far from the cleanest of living abodes, we all got along, so life in this zoo was tolerated out of friendship and family bonds.

The real problem pet, however, turned out to be a small potbellied pig. Having seen some propaganda on The Learning Channel about what great and intelligent pets they made, my pet-loving cousin bought one. It turned out, however, that the pig was EVIL. Although two of the people in the house were pet trainers, this pig refused potty training. He wasn't dumb; he was actually too smart. He decided that *he* was in charge and would go to the bathroom wherever *he* wanted to. He would wait until

The "evil pig" in a post-carpet-soiling slumber.

someone saw him, then stare at them with what came to be known as his "evil eye," and then proceed to do his business. He knew what he was doing.

We cleaned up after him, but he managed to find places to pee that we didn't know about, like behind the fridge or into the heating grate. Needless to say, the smell in our kitchen became quite rank. We were in the middle of suburban Provo, Utah, and it was the dead of winter, so we couldn't take the pig outside.

On top of this, the pig was, well, a pig. There is a reason pigs have a reputation for gluttony. All he ever did was root around for food. Although he had plenty to eat, he was always looking for more. His interaction with people consisted of pushing his snout into you roughly until you fed him. No redeeming qualities. I still tried to love the evil pig, but I soon became the only one who wasn't calling for his well-earned demise.

One night I was awoken by the loud, piercing squeal of the pig in the kitchen. Like an action hero, I sprung, unthinkingly, out of bed to rescue him, thinking he had gotten stuck in the heating grate. I came upon a horrifying sight, however. The twenty-one-foot python had broken out of his Plexiglas cage, clamped its jaws over the pig's snout, and was wrapping itself around that pig—literally squeezing the shit out of him.

My well-thought-out and un-Mormonly response was to yell, "Oh, fuck! Oh, fuck! Oh, fuck!" like a broken record. There wasn't anything that could be done to save the pig at that point, or so I thought.

Hearing my yelling, my pet store cousin came running up the stairs from his room in the basement and, without a thought, grabbed the snake by the head and began to pry its jaws apart with his bare hands. Naively believing our snake expert knew what he was doing, I jumped over the pig fence and grabbed the snake's tail. Fortunately, the snake didn't put up a fight and quickly released its snack. The pig flopped onto the floor and immediately went back to rooting around—back toward the snake. I quickly grabbed him and pulled him up over the divider, whereupon he thanked me by waddling into the living room and urinating on our carpet. Meanwhile, the three other housemates had come out to see what was going on. My hero cousin looked down at his hands, which were, not surprisingly, torn and bloody from the python's teeth, and proceeded to faint from the sight.

For those who are unaware of this, practicing Mormons are required to wear what they call "garments," special long underwear with symbolic marks on them. That evening, with everything happening so fast, no one had been thinking, only reacting. Now we found ourselves staring at one another, taking in the scene. Five guys standing in the kitchen: a hairy one in lobster-themed boxers; three in their sacred long john "garments"—one of whom was smeared with pig shit and lying passed out next to a twenty-one-foot python—and me, much to my chagrin, in a pair of skin-tight turquoise bikini briefs. (The underwear had been a gag gift that I never wore except on this day, as I hadn't done laundry in weeks.)

A few months later, the pig met its demise, and we planned to take him to the butcher's the next day. But it was cold and late, so we left him outside and went to bed. That night, however, there was a heavy snow, and the pig was buried. Being lazy college kids, no one bothered to dig him out and take him away.

About two weeks later, I answered the front door to find two smiling twelve-year-old girls on my doorstep. They said they were in a Mormon youth group and were on an "upgrade scavenger hunt." In this hunt, teams of girls met at the local church, were given some small trinket, and then told to go door to door, continuously trading up for something better, until the time was up and they had to report back to the church to compare items.

Of course, I jokingly offered the girls our frozen pig. After wiping away the snow and rapping my knuckles on it to demonstrate that it was a solidly frozen pigsicle, the girls looked at each other in amazement and politely refused. About twenty minutes later, however, there was a knock at the door. I opened it to see the girls again. "We're so going for the win," they yelled. I bundled up the pigsicle, and the girls dragged it off.

Thankfully, we never heard from anyone inquiring about possible animal cruelty. I can only imagine the reaction of the other girls and their leaders when our frozen pig was rolled out onto the church floor!

—*Brigham Young University*

Alumni Update: This story's author is now a small-town attorney in Maine and has just had his first child.

LESSON LEARNED: The moral is obvious: most college students have enough trouble feeding themselves and cleaning their own soiled quarters, let alone caring for an animal.

House of the Sinking Feeling

What do you get when you combine a group of American college students, a sinkhole, rabid armadillos, sporadic gunfire, and giant cockroaches? Well, it's not the latest B horror movie that's gone straight to DVD. It turns out to be one of the most bizarre roommate issues to occur at Texas A&M University. And since I work in the student housing office, I had a front row seat for it.

One day in late April, I received a phone call from a distressed male senior. He had been rooming with four other young men in an old country house just outside of town. What had once been a cute farmhouse now had all the trappings of a World War II bomb crater. It seems our students had had the misfortune of having their home slide down into a chasm— well, one half the house really; it had broken in two. Adding to their plight, the roommates were being sued by their landlord for the damage. What could have caused such a calamity to these young college kids? Let me give you a little background.

One of our students was majoring in Entomology, or as it is better known, the study of bugs. He had a

Bachelor's degrees in entomology are offered at about thirty colleges in the United States.

little hobby of raising giant cockroaches in a terrarium, basically a roach farm consisting of a fish tank full of dirt and bugs that were nearly the size of cell phones. As fate would have it, during a rather rowdy party, the glass enclosure for the mega-insects was shattered, and the buggers bolted. The insects rapidly multiplied, and soon the students had an infestation.

Texans pride themselves on solving their own problems; it's the cowboy in them. These young scholars were no exception. Another roommate, an Animal Science major, had access to the cockroaches' worst enemy, the dreaded armadillo. The tenants hatched a devious plan. They acquired a few armadillo pups and set them loose around the house to enjoy the roach buffet.

> **Bad Idea Jeans: When one be-haves in a most idiotic fashion. (From a *Saturday Night Live* skit.)**

This was the second shot in a war that would last a full semester. Armadillos also breed at a speedy rate, but not fast enough to keep up with the bugs. Our students now had two infestations roaming inside and outside the house. The critters were found in the beds, the oven, and even coming up through the pipes and into the toilets.

Again, our hotheaded neophytes thought they could handle the newest crisis. In true Wild West fashion, they believed firepower might solve things, namely .22 caliber rifles and twelve-gauge shotguns.

> **The nine-banded armadillo almost always gives birth to four identical pups.**

Most people would have fled the home and called animal control. Not our brave undergraduates. For two weeks they stalked their adversaries. In the process, they expended two hundred rounds of ammunition, causing damage ranging from exploded shower tiles to punctured ceiling fan blades. They claimed that they had "bagged thirty roaches and three armadillos, with another kill unconfirmed."

Yet, the animals still had one last weapon of mass destruction up their furry, scaly sleeves. During the preceding months, the armadillos had expanded their dens, tunneling all over the property, especially under the house. This brought down the party shack one night with a thunderous crash. The boys awakened to find that they had plunged into the armadillo engineering project. Everyone was safe, including the pests who scattered to the four winds after their victory over the awkwardly resourceful humans. After the dust had settled on this extraordinary tale, the students hammered out a plan with the landlord to work off the damages, which totaled more than twenty-five thousand dollars.

To wrap up this creepy-crawly story, all the boys went on to graduate, hopefully a little wiser in the ways of pest control, pet selection, home construction, and urban combat. Yet there are some lingering questions that still haunt me:

Where does one get baby armadillos?
How did they parent-proof this home when Mom and Dad came to visit?
Two hundred rounds of ammunition?

Is thirteen hours of college classes a full load when you have this kind
of free time?

What was the move-out walk-through like at the semester's end?

And most important, did any of these students go into the military?

—Texas A&M University—College Station

LESSON LEARNED: Resourcefulness is a worthy attribute, but there's a point at which you must learn to swallow your pride and ask—nay, beg—for assistance. Ideally, that point will occur before your living room becomes a breeding ground for wild animals.

RELATIONSHIPS

All you need is scented candles, massage oil, and Barry White.
Write that down.
—Van Wilder, *National Lampoon's Van Wilder*

For anyone who's already graduated from college, here's a news flash: today's students are probably hooking up more than you did—even more than you say you did.

For today's college students, relationships are not just about biological urges; they're a whole course of study unto themselves. And judging by the number of stories submitted for this section, "Relationships" is a quite popular major. Students dedicate an excessive amount of time to finding a mate, mating with a mate, and ultimately busting a move on the mate's roommate. After researching his novel *I Am Charlotte Simmons,* author Tom Wolfe called the humping on college campuses a lurid carnival. Well, if Tom read what we've read, he'd promptly stain his white linen suit.

Admittedly it's not all wham-bam-thank-you-what's-your-name. Many college romances do bloom into beautiful, healthy relationships. But who wants to read about those? And don't even get us started on long-distance relationships unless you want to read thirty-two pages of "No, you hang up."

No, folks, this section will not focus on the healthy or even the particularly steamy. These tales represent the less impressive (and often stinkier) side of the dating equation. Welcome to the comedic side of college relationships.

CHAPTER 4

What's Your Sign or Major?

Introduction to the Pickup

Studies declare the death of formal dating on campus. E-mail and IM have removed any need for human interaction. And yet, no bacon can be made without the age-old practice of the pickup.

With emotions and the other half of your twin mattress at stake, the pickup is the most important sales training anyone can experience. Everyone needs to take that first scary step and make the initial pitch. Whether they're selling themselves as sex machines or relationship material, they must stick with it and close the deal before the deed can be done. A valuable lesson for later in life.

Unfortunately for most students—but fortunately for you—many of these transactions end with feet lodged in mouths and tails tucked neatly between legs. Not to mention the occasional head wound.

As long as these pickup artists have as much success with actual pickups as they do with art, we'll always have embarrassing stories to enjoy.

Knockout in a Thong

It started with my parents saying that we were going to spend my college break by all going to Cancún, Mexico, for a "nice, little family vacation."

I was excited to go to Cancún, but not with my family, which included my eleven-year-old sister, Kathy, and my other little sister, Lindy, who is eight. Thankfully, they usually pal around together even though they're three years apart.

From the moment we landed at the airport in Cancún, I was excited to get away from my family and head to the beach. First, we had to go to our hotel and check in. While I was waiting for my parents to get our room keys, I noticed this extremely hot Mexican guy checking me out. I was surprised, because I was sweaty and I didn't exactly look that great.

For the next three days, I kept seeing this great-looking guy. After a while, I decided that since I had an attraction for him, and vice versa, I would follow him around. I grabbed my thong bathing suit (which my mother didn't even know I owned, let alone allow me to wear) and headed down to the beach.

The word "thong" is uttered more than fifty times in rapper Sisqó's lyrical masterpiece, "Thong Song."

My parents had taken my sisters to lunch, so I was alone. I got to the beach just in time to see the guy. I started to follow him, strutting along with my sexiest walk.

We were looking at each other, and I was smiling at him when all of a sudden a Frisbee came flying through the air and hit me in the head! It cut me on the forehead, and the hot guy started to laugh. Some people came over to help me, but I was practically unconscious. Unfortunately, my parents and sisters had come down to the beach when they had finished eating. Thinking I was just a random person, they came over to help.

But when my mom found me in a thong bathing suit with a rather large cut on my head, she was more than a little angry. She started flipping out at me in front of everyone, including the hot guy, who was laughing even harder by then.

The name "Frisbee" is rumored to be derived from the Frisbie Pie Company, whose pie tins were tossed around by Yale students in the 1920s.

Let's just say that my vacation

sucked. And I never saw the hot guy again. Not that it mattered, since I had twenty-seven stitches on my forehead.

—*Lehigh University*

LESSON LEARNED: Accept life's curveballs and roll with the punches. One day this killer Frisbee will be replaced with a pink slip or a surprise "Dear Jane" letter, both of which may also leave you unconscious and half-naked in Mexico.

Irish Accent Thwarted

When I go out to a bar, I usually like to get our group to play "games." Our game playing usually starts with "rock, paper, scissors," and the winner chooses a girl for the loser to hit on. The trick is to make it as difficult as possible for the loser to succeed. To do this, the winner chooses the girl making out with another guy, the angelic beauty who floats instead of walks, or the hard-core lesbian.

Well, this night started out with a loss for me.

"Okay, Clint, where am I going?" I asked, resigned to my unpleasant fate.

My friend was already smiling. I followed his finger to a guy and a girl sitting alone at a table completely enthralled with each other. They were so in love that they were messing with the time-space continuum on that side of the bar. As they stared longingly into each other's eyes, I started my approach and began concocting a plan for pulling off the most terrible cock block in the history of Waldo's Campus Tavern.

> Waldo's is the closest bar to the Western Michigan campus— a mere couple hundred yards from the student recreation center.

I managed to get the girl's attention, smiled, and approached her as if I'd known her my whole life. This was definitely going to take an Irish accent.

"EEEIIIYYY! HOWARYA!!" I bellowed with jolly Irish cheer.

It usually took people a couple of sentences to pick up on the accent. I began making rapid-fire chitchat, not allowing the girl a chance to ask who I was, and to give the impression that I would be offended if she didn't remember me.

The boyfriend wasn't amused from the start. "I don't believe you're from Ireland," he said, glaring.

"Why da fook not?" I held the cocky Irish bar-fighting smile I'd seen so many times across the pond.

"Ha ha, I'm just kidding!" he said, looking at his beer.

I kept talking with the girl while the guy's anger festered. Eventually I glanced up at my friends and got an approving thumbs-up. Enough was enough. I felt like a prick.

I looked back at the girl. "Well, I'm going to go now. Nice meeting you," I said in my boring Midwest Honkey accent.

I walked back over to the group. The couple watched my hearty reception. I'm sure they were big fans at that point.

For the next game, I had to play against someone else. "Rock, paper, scissors." Damn, I lost again!

This time, I was sent to the floating goddess of beauty. I wiped the drool from my chin and started my approach, concocting a plan. Again, I knew this required an Irish accent.

"EEEEIIYY!! HOWARYA!!" I said, approaching her with my well-practiced smile.

She stood there smiling as if she knew something I didn't. What could it be? This was usually the point at which I'd start talking so the girl wouldn't have time to ask questions. But she was shaking her head "no." I could hear my friends' bellowing laughter from the other side of the bar.

"Whatcha shakin' yer head for?" I asked her.

"You've tried this on me before." She was still smiling and tapping her foot with her arms crossed.

"Ahh, msohrry?" I looked at her like she was crazy.

"Yeah, and I know your friends from high school," she said, and then started running off the names of the people in my posse. I managed to just keep shaking my head "no" like she was crazy.

"Your name is Patrick. We've been through this fake Irish thing before . . ."

I kept shaking my head while thinking about when I'd met this girl. Then it clicked. I'd done this to her at a bar, gotten her number, then called her the next day, forgetting about

> Get the Heisman: To get one's advances rejected. From the stiff-arm pose of the Heisman trophy.

the accent. When she asked me what had happened to my accent, I quickly remembered and told her I was a hybrid.

Now I kept the accent anyway: "It's not all my fault. You never called me back either!"

She looked down at her beer and quietly said, "Now you have a booger hanging out of your nose, too."

I reached up to shuck the ripe crystal of mucus inconspicuously. But Mr. Snot McTweety had other plans. Like a baby spider in *Charlotte's Web,* it released its snot string web into the air—landing very conspicuously on the edge of the table.

The girl walked back to her group of friends to a loud hearty reception.

A worthy opponent.

—*Western Michigan University*

LESSON LEARNED: Macking on someone, like any worthy life endeavor, calls for using any means necessary—even assuming a false identity. But beware, the light of honesty will shine on your lies. In short, a real booger beats a fake broguer any day.

Faith Under Fire

Like many people who went to school in the wake of the Reagan era, my collegiate experience was dramatically shaped by the zero-tolerance mandate known as "Just Say No." And though this tagline was originally conceived with a specific war in mind, it was eventually pounded into the broader collective consciousness, functioning as a fear-inspiring catchall that condemned every recreational reason for attending college in the first place: drugs, rock and roll, and especially sex. In today's era of *Girls Gone Wild* and dorm-based Webcams that rival Jenna Jameson's best work, it's hard to imagine how sexless university life was in the late 1980s.

Or, maybe it was just me.

Whatever the case, I spent the better part of four years at the University of Michigan huddled in various libraries, trying to comprehend nineteenth-century political theory and frustrated by the fact that my life was nothing like the steamy cinematic representations of college that had defined my adolescence. Where were the hedonistic, vodka-soaked orgies? How did one locate the treasure trove of nymphomaniacal sorority sisters? And why was every woman in sight draped in an oversize double-ply Champion sweatshirt that covered her body from neck to kneecap? If these were my salad days, I was sorely in need of more tossing.

The few experiences I did have that bordered on being worthy of a *Penthouse* Forum letter turned out more like an Abbott and Costello routine than anything from *Animal House,* as one example from my sophomore year illustrates. Somehow I had wrangled a date with Clara, a perky freshman focusing on Comparative Literature. We had met through mutual friends, who suggested that Clara had found my affinity for cardigan sweaters charming. This seemed unlikely, but I decided it was as good an excuse as any to ask her out.

While the date started out with a modest effort at a romantic dinner, most of the evening was spent at a friend's "progressive" party. This defined not the politics of the affair but rather the fact that each room of the house featured a different drink, concocted by that room's host. The goal, it seemed, was to "progress" from room to room while ingesting as many different types of alcohol as possible—such that drinks floated upon one another like an eighty-proof liquid layer cake. Before we'd completed a tour of the first floor, Clara was tanked, and I wasn't far behind. And that's when she heard the melodic call of George Michael.

George Michael was born Georgios Kyriacos Panayiotou.

The fact that a nation of college boys had to put up with the saccharine sounds of the former Wham! frontman in order to try to get laid is an indication of how vacant the cultural landscape was at that time. Nonetheless, the album *Faith* is what got the booties shaking in those days, and even an Exeter alum with feminist leanings like Clara was not immune to its charms. We spent the rest of the evening getting our groove on, and things seemed to be *progressing* nicely.

After a quick dash to a local diner called The Brown Jug, we reached the less-than-pristine comfort of my living room. While we'd been together for nearly five hours, we'd had few opportunities to really get to know each other, and I was interested in digging a little deeper. In the days before cell phones and instant messaging, college students were forced to actually have face-to-face conversations, and this was an example of that old-fashioned practice.

With genuine intrigue, I asked Clara about her hometown, her classes, and her favorite foods. I was by no means smooth, but I did have a reporter's gift for the initial interviewing process. Her reply led me to believe that we were not quite on the same page.

"You know, if you think you're going to talk me into bed tonight, you're wrong," she said, adding an icy layer to the warm mood I had tried to establish with the obligatory incense and candlelight setup.

The date, it seemed, was over. Whether she was correct about my intentions or not—I was a twenty-year-old male, after all—I was taken aback by the allegation. I was also a little confused. Was her disinterest personal, or had I simply failed to make a persuasive enough argument? And might there be another night when I would be able to talk her into bed? She seemed too drunk for a semantic debate, so I let it go, choosing to confront a more pressing issue: how to get her home.

> Face-to-face conversations are when at least two people communicate within close proximity, unmediated by e-mail, IMs, or cell phones. It went out of style in 1996.

Her residence was a twenty-five-minute walk from my house under the most sober of circumstances, and my car was in the shop. Still, I insisted that I drive her back, so I grabbed a set of keys that belonged to my housemate Michael. Few women could resist the charms of Michael's 1979 Chrysler New Yorker, with its faux-walnut dashboard and two-tone paint job. Apparently, the sedan's smooth ride was more than Clara could handle, because by the time we reached her dorm, she was sound asleep.

I walked her to the front door, explained the situation to the security guard, and carried her up to her room, depositing her onto a bunk bed. I tore a piece of paper from her Trapper Keeper and left a brief note on top of her toiletry bucket, explaining how she had arrived home. I assumed I'd never hear from her again.

I was wrong. She called the next morning to thank me, and apologized for her outburst. She'd had some tough experiences with "upperclassmen," and she was a bit guarded. I appreciated her maturity but admitted that she was not entirely wrong about my intentions. We decided to chalk it up as a funny story.

And while I never did talk her into bed, Clara and I became friends. One day, a couple of months after our date, we were walking across the main quadrangle, when we bumped into a group of her girlfriends, and I was introduced to the gaggle. A few days later I received a funny, anonymous, hand-delivered invitation to a crush party. As I learned when I showed up at the designated address, my crusher turned out to be Alison, one of Clara's closest friends, whom I'd met briefly that day on the quad. The party turned out to be a fortuitous starting point—Alison and I would date for the next four years. And though we eventually broke up after graduation, the memories inspire the nostalgic fondness that often follows in the wake of first love.

Had Clara just said yes the night of the fateful progressive affair, it's doubtful that I would have met Alison. My history would have taken another course—not better or worse, but certainly different. As it turned out, the fact that Clara gave me a firm "no" allowed us to pursue a friendship, which eventually led me to Alison. And while my college days weren't as wild as I'd originally imagined they might be, the years were memorable and full of important relationships, and there is little about them that I would change. As George Michael understood, sometimes you just gotta have faith, faith, faith.

—*University of Michigan*

Alumni Update: Peter Hyman, a former *Vanity Fair* staffer, is the author of *The Reluctant Metrosexual: Dispatches from an Almost Hip Life.* He has written for *The New York Times, The Wall Street Journal, The New York Observer, Details, Spin,* and various other publications. He blogs with fervent attention to grammar at Pdhyman.com/blog.

LESSON LEARNED: Accepting rejection with a touch of class and dignity can pay unexpected dividends in the long run, from gaining a new love interest to gaining a new appreciation for George Michael.

Don't Drink the Punch

I came to college by myself, in the middle of a hurricane no less. I was a transfer student, and I had all my stuff in a storage unit downtown. So I decided to spend my day walking around the town and campus to get better acquainted with my new surroundings. Along the way, I looked for that infamous house party. You know, the no-cover party with the red cups and the kegs, the ice luge and the beer bongs and the people screaming from the roof. I figured there had to be something big going on somewhere.

Eventually I got my wish.

I was on a side street off the main road to campus when I saw it. Girls and guys were standing around the front yard and blocking the sidewalk, drinking out of red and blue plastic cups. There was a band playing on the terrace roof. Guitars and bongo drums. The perfect chance to get boozed up before meeting my new roommates.

As I slowed down, a girl caught my arm. She handed me her plastic cup. She was leaning into me and dancing a little, but not looking at my eyes. "Do you want to party?" she yelled, arching her back against me, still dancing.

Finding my hand, she took it and pulled me past a group of guys. I wondered if she was one of theirs. Probably, but I didn't care. Inside the house, the band music was louder, and people stood in groups laughing and talking, red and blue cups in their hands. The girl took the cup back from me and let go of my hand, her fingers sliding across mine as she walked away.

"Don't go anywhere," she whispered into my ear, and my hand dropped to my side, a snapped synapse.

When she came back she had two cups.

"Blue for the boys," she giggled as she put her arm around my shoulder.

She asked me my name and where I was from, how I came to go to school here, and what my major was. All the while, she brushed against my shoulder with hers, and whenever I said something that made her laugh, she would touch me on my arm. I felt a pressure begin in the front of my jeans, and kept on smiling.

"So, I guess this is where I ask you?" she said.

I wasn't sure what she meant, but my imagination was racing with the possibilities.

"You know . . . ," she said, and stood directly in front of me. She looked into my eyes, head tilted a little, a piece of her hair hanging in front of her eyes. She blew it out of the corner of her mouth, and in a second I thought I would kiss her.

"So . . . have you been saved?" she asked, her head bent forward and eyes widening as if the question were something the two of us had been dancing around all night.

My cup was to my lips. I took a sip . . . and almost choked.

Suddenly I could hear the band playing through the ceiling, the acoustic guitar and the bongo drums. The vocals haunting and familiar. I looked out through the glass doors to the lawn and the sidewalk. I could see all the kids with their hands raised toward the sky or toward the music, and they were singing. I looked down into my cup. I was drinking punch. It was a goddamn church party!

I ran all the way home.

Even now that I'm almost done with college, that first day of school is something I'll always remember. It

> **Team Jesus:** A group of fervent religious students who proselytize and preach with extreme passion and sometimes little tact.

was the big kick in the ass that I'd deserved since the day I first started funneling beers and skipping classes.

And when I need that extra kick in the ass that tells me, "Maybe it's time to grow up and out of this lifestyle," I see that girl looking at me over her fruit punch with her goody-girl, no-sex-before-the-honeymoon future-red-state-housewife bedroom eyes, and I think: I guess I needed that.

—*University of South Carolina*

LESSON LEARNED: Looks like this author overanalyzed the lesson for himself. Well done. There's something cockle-warming about Mr. Smooth getting punk'd by Team Jesus. Maybe that's just our cockles.

CHAPTER 5

Creeping Creeps

An Overview of Stalking Strategies

Anyone who accuses college students of being lazy hasn't seen them stalk. There's nothing lazy about filling up someone's voice mail with hang-ups or showing up unexpectedly in the middle of the night, then still finding time to talk behind their backs. That's multitasking, Holmes.

It's important to learn in life that you should never take no for an answer. Even if that "no" is surrounded by, "you are hereby forbidden to come NO closer than one hundred feet of my client." Part of the college relationship game is the pursuit. And pursue these students do, showing the dedication to their single-minded and totally creepy goal.

Ironically, stalking is rarely listed on the opposite sex's top one hundred thousand possible turn-ons. So while admirable in their perseverance and brashness, our stalkers often end up dateless and empty-handed—except for the crowbar they've just used to smash your windshield in.

So if you're considering a career in campus stalking, we recommend the following stories as required reading—and as a warning.

Trashing Tampa Psycho

Spring break has a rich tradition of injecting fun and adventure into the lives of hardworking college students. This is merely one of those stories.

I'd done the insanity of Ft. Lauderdale the previous year, so we decided we'd hit Tampa. Besides, Phil's brother was a manager at the Tampa Marriott, so we could crash at his place for free. The five of us drove straight through from Durham, New Hampshire, to Tampa.

That first night there, we headed out to a packed club. After less than an hour at the club, Phil was dancing with some chick. Phil never wasted any time with the ladies . . .

The next night we went to a house party. And lo and behold, there was the same chick. Turned out she worked at the Tampa Marriott. So Phil and the girl once again hit it off big time, to the point where our boy didn't come home that night. We next saw him late the following morning—when he turned up at the apartment pale, shaky, and a bit freaked out.

When we asked him what was up, he just said, "This girl, man . . . she's *strange*. You know that Eastwood flick *Play Misty for Me*? She's that strange."

> The 1971 stalker thriller *Play Misty for Me* was Clint Eastwood's first film as a director.

And at that very moment, I swear, the phone rang. It was the girl, of course. Phil mouthed, "I'm not here," and we got rid of her. But from that point on, she called every thirty minutes for the next three days!

Phil was freaking out. He whined about being stalked, and he started to become unglued. It was clear that this girl suffered from some sort of emotional maladjustment.

The next time the phone rang, Tim took matters into his own hands. Pretending to be Rick, he answered the phone and said: "This isn't Phil. This is his brother, Rick . . . your boss at the Marriott. And if you call here one more time, you're fired."

That night, we borrowed Rick's primo decked-out Nissan Z, drove out to the Seminole reservation, and hit the jai alai fronton. It was about 2:00 A.M. when we started heading back. We were jammed into the Z: Tim was driving, Mark was hovering over the stick, Phil was curled up under the hatch, and I was riding "shotgun." We were headed down the highway and . . . WHAM!

There was a hideous noise, and the car careened across the lane and banged into the barrier. Tim was freaking out yet managed somehow to keep the car under control and continue driving.

> American Datsun/Nissan Z sales surpassed the one-million sales mark in the early nineties, becoming the all-time bestselling sports car.

Then, from the back, Phil said in a low voice, "Jesus H." We looked where he was looking.

It was her. The stalker girl. She was driving a station wagon and slamming it into us. It was like something out of *Mannix*. She kept yanking the wheel to the side and banging into us. She was possessed.

Both cars were doing like seventy. We were approaching an exit and, at the last second, Tim spun the wheel. Thankfully, the girl missed the exit. We barreled down the off-ramp, blew through the light, and skidded to a stop in an empty lot in a cloud of dust. After we made sure no one was dead, we tried to get our bearings. We were across the street from a place called The Bloody Eye Bar, in the nastiest Cuban neighborhood in Tampa . . . at 2:00 A.M. with no idea how to get back.

People seemed to come from out of nowhere. And they weren't pleased. It seems that when we flew off the expressway, we just missed a "working girl" on the corner. Several young men started running toward our car, yelling and gesturing wildly.

Tim put the car back in gear, and we flew over the curb and out into the street. After much backtracking, we finally found our apartment building and pulled into the lot. I jumped out of the car to inspect the damage. The Z looked as if it had been played by a Caribbean steel drum band. I was standing in the beams of the headlights, holding my head in a gesture of sheer disbelief and looking at Tim, who was still behind the wheel, when I noticed Tim. He looked funny. What was that look in his eye? Fear? Panic?

He suddenly put the Z into reverse and hit the gas.

I was thinking, "What the hell is he doing?" when all of a sudden the Freak Chick ran past me with a big metal bar. As she ran, she clutched the bar high over her head, screamed bloody murder, and brought it down right on the hood of the Z. My three University of New Hampshire buddies still in the car also screamed. Then Tim put the car in drive and got out of there, vanishing into the night.

Still holding the metal bar, the girl turned toward me. I just stood there, not knowing quite what to do. In that moment, I looked around me to see that every car in the parking lot had had its windshield smashed. The girl said to me, almost as if it were a conversation starter, "I'm gonna kill you all."

And then, right on cue, the police showed up and took her away.

Like I said, spring break injects fun and adventure into the lives of hard-working college students. Now I'd add the fear of God to that list, too.

> Mike Myers starred in the sleeper 1993 comedy *So I Married an Axe Murderer.*

—*University of New Hampshire*

LESSON LEARNED: Our psycho stalker can teach us a lot about determination, drive, and total lunacy. She demonstrates a try-try-and-try-again work ethic. On the other hand, her psychosis proves that movies are right—crazy villains are unstoppable.

Grad Student Stalker

During the summer orientation before school started, my first year at App State, I met a grad student named Brad. He seemed to be extremely interested in me, but I told him that I was very much in love with my boyfriend, who also goes to school up here. He seemed cool with that. So before I returned home, for the last few weeks, we exchanged e-mails.

Every day, Brad sent me at least three different e-mails—actually letters, not just forwards. At first I thought it was a little sweet that someone could be so interested in me, but after a while I started to get worried. When I finally got up to school, Brad found out my number and started calling at least four times a day. I eventually had to have my poor roommate start lying for me.

> The National Center for the Victims of Crime reports that one out of every twelve women will be stalked during her lifetime.

A few weeks into the year, I was in my dorm's lobby talking with my roommate about Brad, and an upperclassman overheard us. Apparently, Brad had stalked her the previous year. I couldn't believe it! He had followed the same pattern with her: friendly and sweet at first, then more and more obsessive over time.

I went right over to my boyfriend's dorm room. And a few minutes after I arrived, the phone rang. My boyfriend answered it. It was Brad. (The fact that Brad didn't know my boyfriend hadn't stopped him.)

"I know Susan is there! Let me speak to her. I know she is over there!" At that point, I knew we were dealing with a total psycho! My boyfriend basically told him to "fuck off." But I should have known that wouldn't be the last I'd hear from Brad.

As I was walking back to my room alone that night (not the smartest thing to do), I heard someone behind me. At first I ignored it and just picked up the pace. Then I suddenly turned around to confront . . . guess who! I sprinted toward the nearest streetlight and then straight for my dorm. All the while, Brad kept calling out my name. I never looked back.

After that, Brad left me alone—no more phone calls, no following me around, nothing. A few weeks later, when I'd come back to my room after classes one day, that all changed. I went to open the door and found it unlocked. Since my roommate often left the door unlocked, it didn't really register with me that something might be wrong. Inside the room, I started to change my clothes, turning up my music and singing along.

Suddenly, I noticed out of the corner of my eye in the mirror someone sitting on my bunk bed. I started to grab something quick to get dressed, and as I turned around, Brad was standing face-to-face with me. He was very calm. He told me I had an awesome body. I wanted to scream but was unable to utter a single sound. He leaned in to kiss me, and I pushed him away. I threw him out, while also screaming to my RA, who

According to criminal lawyer Andrej Bajuk, this grad student's actions meet the definition of stalking: a misdemeanor. The law in North Carolina saves him from the felony charge of burglary.

(as it turned out) was another of Brad's former stalking victims. She kicked him out and called the campus police.

Thankfully, I haven't seen or heard from Brad since!

—*Appalachian State University*

LESSON LEARNED: Anyone too nice to be true probably is. There's a corollary to this: No guy is just cool with being friends. If he is, he's either a potential Brad or a potential shopping buddy, if you know what we mean (not that there's anything wrong with that).

For the Love and Stalking of Martin

Martin had the grizzled-yet-chiseled look of a model in the J.Crew winter catalog. You know, the twinkly-eyed guy with the strategically placed stubble, with a Christmas tree slung over his strong, flannel-clad shoulders, heading back to the cabin in time to cuddle and build bookshelves.

Although he had been cuddling me plenty, it really was still too early in our relationship to expect carpen-

J.Crew has a catalog circulation of over eighty million.

try projects. However, that hadn't stopped me, completely intoxicated by Martin's exotic East Coast Ivy League–ness and taut crew-team torso, from plunging headfirst into stupid-girl land.

What sealed the deal on my delirium, though, was that on top of being a hunk and a Ph.D. candidate, Martin also drove a motorcycle when he came by for nightly nookie. And who can resist a hot, smart bad boy? Certainly not me!

So it's no surprise I found myself drunk on rum and Cokes and pressing my friends for possible explanations when he suddenly stopped calling me after just a few weeks.

It wasn't like he'd promised to call, because he hadn't. That was part of what made him such a bad boy, just phoning out of the blue and showing up like a dark, dirty knight.

It's just that up until that point, I'd been too flush with the soft-focus memories of wine and candle wax to question why he'd always had to leave to feed his dog. Or why I'd never met his friends.

At the bar that night, I checked my voice mail so many times the buttons started to wear off my cell phone. It was time for my friend Tracy to drive me home—though not without first doing a "drive-spy" of Martin's place.

I could feel my heart in my throat as Tracy's blue Geo sliced through the eerie darkness of Martin's street. We slowed to a near stop across the street from his white A-frame, and I threw a musty towel over my head to conceal my identity. I considered the empty jack-o'-lantern yellowness of his front windows and waited for something, anything, to happen.

As the car circled the block and rolled toward Martin's house for the third time, the icy-hot tingle in my spine rushed up to my ears. I just had to see *something*.

Like any good friend, Tracy killed the headlights, veered a sharp right, and gassed her Geo up Martin's steep driveway, narrowly missing his mailbox. I craned my neck over the dashboard for a closer look. Suddenly, I heard Martin's dog barking. Panic, and Captain Morgan, surged up my esophagus. "Go!" I cried.

But when Tracy shifted into reverse and hit the gas, the car wouldn't budge. She had overshot the pavement and had wedged the car's left tires into a deep, muddy crevice inches from the driveway.

I knew I couldn't be found stuck at a forty-five-degree angle in Martin's yard. I flung myself out the passenger door and spilled onto the glassy street, my heels clack-clacking on the pavement as I ran toward the tangle of trees by the railroad tracks. Rubbery-smelling smoke turned the blackness milky gray as Tracy stomped on the gas pedal over and over. On the other side of the cottonwoods, I waited for a freight car to Mexico.

Then, like a big white panther, a police car stole up beside me. The policeman, youngish with kind eyes, asked if I'd seen a fire.

Not to be taken for an arsonist, I caught a ride with him back to Martin's house, where Tracy was cramming dirty laundry from her backseat under the tires for traction. She rose from behind the car clutching a wad of mucky socks and told the cop she'd gotten stuck trying to turn around.

I'm not sure how that explained me in the trees, but the cop bought it. The red and blue lights of his squad car danced over Martin's white clapboard as we waited for a tow truck.

By the time the largest tow truck I'd ever seen growled up to us, I'd nearly rediscovered Catholicism while praying Martin wouldn't see me. The truck was freakishly huge. Instead of dragging the car, it actually lifted the car up over the earth and deposited it onto the street. Loudly.

Still, a light never came on at Martin's. No one ran onto the lawn with a shotgun. And as if that weren't miraculous enough, the cop also let us drive home drunk.

It was, it turned out, a great night to be a dumb girl.

—*University of Texas—Austin*

Alumni Update: "Martin and I went out for a few more weeks, but eventually he just disappeared. Today, I'm a copywriter in New York City and am engaged to a man whom I did not have to stalk, thank you very much."

LESSON LEARNED: If you take anything away from this, remember that obsessive behavior is rarely smooth. It's nearly impossible to maintain any element of cool when you're stalking someone, painting your chest for a local team, or waiting outside the courthouse for your single-gloved idol.

CHAPTER 6

Screwing Up Screwing

Contemporary Studies in Unromantic Moments

There's a fine line between steamy and stinky, between bliss and blister. This line seems to get crossed every night on creaky bunks across the country. When you consider how awkward the typical college hookup is, the term "fooling around" should be replaced with "fumbling around."

We'd love to say that college kids are simply bad in the sack. Unfortunately, the truth is that they're screwing so much they simply have more chances of screwing it up. And they don't mind bragging about it on a website.

Studying these unfortunate acts of fornication is critical because knowing what *not* to do is almost more important than doing it right. Think about it: tales of bedroom bloopers make their way around campus quicker than a naked frat pledge who's lost a bet.

And when you get a little older, and your nesting gland starts kicking in, you'll want to know that you've gotten the most embarrassing and possibly fatal hookups out of your system.

So consider regarding these stories about what not to say and where not to do it as a kind of *Scared Straight* for the bedroom (with fewer pissed-off prisoners).

The Odds Are Against Me

I transferred from a small college to a larger one closer to home. The weekend before classes started at my new school, my best friend and I decided to check out the local clubs.

We were having a great time mingling and dancing when who should I see but the guy I had had a crush on during my entire high school career. He was a sexy, popular senior when I was a mere freshman, so I had never actually gotten up the nerve to talk to him. Still, it was nice just to ogle him from a distance. That evening, I shot playful glances at him when I thought he wasn't looking, until *he* walked up to *me*.

"You look familiar," he said. "Want to dance?"

Did I want to dance?

So we danced. Then, after a quick smooch, he invited me and my friend back to his apartment to hang out with him and his friends. Elated, I practically skipped to my car. As I was a little tipsy, my best friend drove my car, and the whole way over there she kept repeating to me, "Don't do anything you wouldn't do sober."

Me? Act irresponsibly while under the influence? Never. But me acting irresponsibly under the influence of a crush? That was a little more likely.

After a couple of hours at his apartment, as lover boy and I continued drinking, my "responsible" friend took my car keys and told me she'd come back to get me in the morning.

Soon after she left, he and I were stumbling to his bedroom, making out. Before long, clothes started coming off. He was a less-than-fabulous kisser, but I wasn't really worried.

And then he started doing something with his mouth that was simply unacceptable: talking. At first it was mild stuff: "Oooh, do you like that?" and "Yeah, baby. I love it when you do that."

I was literally biting my bottom lip to keep from hee-hawing in the poor guy's face. I was doing pretty well—stroking his member and praying that if I kept quiet he would get the hint and stop talking.

Then, a fly landed on the camel's back.

> Down the basement
> Lock the cellar door
> And baby
> Talk dirty to me
> —Poison, "Talk Dirty to Me"

"Whose dick is it?" he asked me.

I pretended I hadn't heard him. Oh God, make this stop.

"Whose dick is it?" he repeated more forcefully. "WHOSE DICK IS IT?"

That was it. I couldn't take it anymore.

"Umm . . . mine?" I ventured.

All the pent-up hilarity came gushing out, and I was screaming with laughter. My high school crush didn't find it quite so funny. His look of embarrassment was enough to have sent me bolting out the door.

The only problem was that my best friend had my car, and I wasn't really fit to drive anyway. I was stranded. In an act of desperation, I rolled over and pretended that I had passed out. My talkative friend followed suit. In the morning, I crept out of bed and dialed my friend six or seven times until she finally answered.

"Come get me *now*," I pleaded.

> I learned that silence is golden, and bad porn is confusing young men into assigning ownership of their members. But what I *really* want to know is, whose dick was it? That question may plague me forever.
>
> —story author Amanda Leigh Coll

The author during happier—and less confusing—times.

When she pulled up, I *ran* to my car. After several horrified minutes of silence, I told her the whole story. When we'd both finished laughing our heads off, she brought up something I hadn't considered.

"What if you have a class with him?"

"Not likely," I said. "I mean, what are the odds of that?"

What were the odds indeed? That Monday, who should sit down next to me in Music Appreciation but my high school crush and five of his frat boy friends?

My only comfort was that he didn't seem to remember me, which made sense considering how drunk we had both been. I spent many Music Appreciation class periods mulling over that night . . . that horrible night when I learned some crushes are better left unattained.

—*University of Southern Mississippi*

LESSON LEARNED: You can't take back words, in any situation. So fight the urge to say something freaky-deeky in the heat of passion. If you can't stop yourself, just keep the zipper on your leather gimp mask closed tight.

Fiery Passion

Throughout high school, I had zero success with women. My physical disability and superior academic performance basically made me the poster child for wallflowers everywhere. Needless to say, I was thrilled when, shortly after arriving at the University of Nevada—Las Vegas, I met Katie, who had the same disability, and an academic standing near my own. She also had the biggest boobs I had ever seen.

We quickly became a couple. We delighted in kissing, hugging, and snuggling both in public and in private. Things were moving slowly, but neither of us really cared. We were both just ecstatic to have finally found love.

One night in the spring, Katie called about 1:00 A.M., begging me to come see her immediately. So, of course I hightailed it over, fully expecting a late-night snack of coed served warm.

At first, everything went according to plan. Katie met me at her door completely nude. After closing the door, she sat in my lap (I use a wheelchair), and gave me my first-ever French kiss. Then, she stretched out horizontally across my lap, and gave me free rein to kiss her everywhere. After several minutes, the words I had waited for since we had first met finally came: "Let's do it."

Quicker than I could say, "Hell yeah," we were on her bed rolling around. The shy, quiet girl I had known turned out to be a crazed passion kitten under the covers. Just as we were climaxing, however, the trouble began.

> "Let's do it" is also an important line in *Animal House* and is explained in greater detail in the popular course Movies That Frat Guys Quote Way Too Much.

As a prank, some idiot had set a small fire in one of the dorm rooms. Within moments, the sprinklers had drenched everything. This was disconcerting enough, but next came the ear-splitting wail of the fire alarm. Believing it to be a prank, Katie and I merely huddled under the soaked sheets and prepared to have at it again. Then Katie's door opened to reveal a soggy and none-too-pleased resident assistant shouting, "There's a fire on the floor, and it's spreading. Get the hell out now!" Primal lust instantly gave way to self-preservation as we hurriedly dressed and exited the building. Thankfully, nobody was injured.

Unfortunately, that was the beginning of the end of our relationship. We quickly grew apart, and broke up a few weeks later. Still, I am grateful for the night when I realized that even those who don't fit in can occasionally have some real fun.

—*University of Nevada—Las Vegas*

LESSON LEARNED: No matter how awkward and outcast you may feel, just know that there is someone out there who is perfect for you— perfect for you to fumble around with during an embarrassing hookup session.

Do the Hustle

It was just another Wednesday night on the prowl. After hitting it off with a cute girl, I ended up in my dorm room with her. We were in my tiny dorm bed, going at it pretty hard, when I noticed the door slowly crack open.

Out of the corner of my eye, I saw my roommate silently creep into the room. It was late, and he had early classes the next day, so I was not surprised to see him doing this. The girl in my bed didn't notice him, and he quietly hurried into his bed (just a few feet from mine) and threw the covers over himself.

A half hour later, my "date" and I were exhausted after a rigorous session. She sat up in bed and faced me. "Do you have some boxers and a T-shirt that I can sleep in?" she asked.

At that point, being a despicable male, I started thinking about how small the dorm bed was and how uncomfortable it was for two people to share it. I decided it would be much nicer if, even though she was a cute girl, she took off for the night. "Why don't you go find your friends?" I suggested. "They're probably worried about you; they don't even know where you are."

She shrugged and said, "That's okay. They know I can take care of myself."

> **Ass Hug:** Cuddling all night with someone. Also known as spooning or fancy sleeping.

After a few more subtle attempts to get rid of her, I was getting frustrated, so I made one more stab: "Seriously, I think you should go let them know what's up. We can always hang out later."

She paused, looking like she was trying to make up her mind. I saw that she was considering leaving, so I tried to prod her along.

"Come on," I said, quietly clapping my hands. "Let's hustle!"

That stopped her dead in her tracks. She looked at me in disbelief and said, "Did you just tell me to 'hustle'?"

> The hustle became an international dance craze in 1975, following Van McCoy and the Soul City Symphony's song "The Hustle."

Just then, my roommate (whom I had completely forgotten about) burst out roaring with laughter. The girl gave a little jump, then shot me an angry look. She quickly gathered up her clothes, dressed, and left without a word, slamming the door behind her.

I saw her the next weekend at a party and tried to talk to her, but she wouldn't even speak to me. Damn.

—*Northern Arizona University*

LESSON LEARNED: Getting someone to leave is a tricky proposition—whether it's your bed, your office, or your chichi dinner party. But the phrase "let's hustle" should only be used by guys in tight polyester shorts with whistles around their necks.

AUTHORITY

Any acceptance of authority is the very denial of truth.
—Jiddu Krishnamurti, Indian religious leader

Developing a healthy disrespect for authority in all shapes, sizes, and forms is an integral part of the college experience. Whether your cause is great or small, this is the time for you to stand up and shout, in the words of Rage Against the Machine, "Fuck you, I won't do what you told me."

With teachers, parents, cops, and the administration around, there's no shortage of targets for college students' collective ire. Critics might suggest this behavior to be a sort of misguided rebellion, executed largely by well-to-do students who will soon become part of the very same corrupt system with which they're clashing. But we prefer to look at this glorious state of rebellion as a breeding ground for free and creative thinkers. Once you're in the real world, you'll have to fight through plenty of red tape. Through a little collegiate trial and error, you can learn when the rules should be bent, broken, or painstakingly detailed in a letter to the campus newspaper.

Whether you're a rebel with a cause or one without a clue, you'll enjoy this healthy dose of stories extolling the virtues of tussling with authority.

CHAPTER 7

The Parent Trap

Psychology of the Parent-Child Relationship

As the Fresh Prince Will Smith so acutely observed, "Parents just don't understand." Never is the generational gap in understanding greater than when a child exits the safe confines of home for the wild, cheesy-poster-covered walls of college.

Having invested tens of thousands in their child's "education," parents often go to sleep with sweet visions of their offspring studying long hours and falling asleep on their pillow with textbook in hand. For the lucky parents, that's exactly the case. But in some situations, the book is replaced with a beer, the pillow with the body of a coed.

When parents visit their children at school and see what their tuition's *really* been buying, the clash of perception versus reality can be explosive. And, in our opinion, that clash makes for some amazing stories. It also gives students a chance to exercise emergency problem-solving skills and the damage-control methods that will come in handy in the years ahead. You try hiding six bottles of liquor, someone else's underwear, and two failed tests in under a minute and you'll see what we mean.

We hope these tales of parent-child (mis)relations will help bring one generation closer to the other. If not, they should at least make for some fun reading.

Horny and Hiding

It was a typical weekend night: drinking at the bars, chatting with the ladies. I even managed to convince a girl that it would be in her best interest to take me back to her place after last call. We grabbed one last drink, closed out the tab, and proceeded to the girl's apartment. One thing led to another, and I was thinking a hookup was a done deal. Not so fast. She informed me that her family was coming into town the next day. No problem. I assured her that I always woke up early, and I would be out of there before the arrival of her family. Upstairs to her apartment we went.

The next morning I was awakened by the sound of OutKast's "Hey Ya" blaring from the girl's cell phone on the nightstand. I went from dead sleep to WIDE FUCKING AWAKE almost instantaneously. The girl silenced the phone by hitting the talk button and inquired sleepily, "Hey, are you guys on your way?"

There was a moment of silence.

Suddenly her face erupted into an expression of outright terror and disbelief. With eyes bulging, she looked right at me as she managed a calm reply, "Yeah, that's fine. Just come on up. I just need to shower and get ready. See you in a minute."

Then she turned to me. "Holy shit! They are coming up to the door RIGHT NOW! Shit! They were supposed to call me an hour before they got here!"

The video for "Hey Ya" is based on the Beatles' landmark appearance on *The Ed Sullivan Show* on February 9, 1964.

Needing to act fast, I thought to myself, "Okay, no problem, I'll just grab my personal belongings and get the hell out of here." Right then the doorbell rang. "Shit, you've got to hide NOW!" she yelled before jumping up and running from the bedroom.

I opened her closet door only to find that it was filled to capacity with her clothes, shoes, etc. I started to curse my bad luck and the fact that she had so many damn shoes. But I didn't have time to dwell on her shoe collection—I needed to find a place to hide. And fast. The closet was no good, so where? The bathroom? No, what if a family member needed to use it? Little kids and old people always have to use the facilities on road trips.

Under the bed! I could hear her greeting her family downstairs. I dove under the bed, dragging my shit and jeans along with me. It was a pretty tight fit, but I was fully concealed.

Her door opened. From under the bed, my only visual reference came from a one-inch gap between the bottom of her bed skirt and the floor. Wonderful. I saw her unshod feet followed by other feet, these with shoes. A pair of leather loafers: that would be Dad. Some child-size athletic shoes: there's little brother. Two pairs of women's casual shoes, one with a pair of chubby ankles protruding: we had Mom and Grandma as well.

Fine, no problem. I'd just chill there until they left. It's not as if they were going to go snooping around under her bed, right? My clothes were under there with me. I had flushed the condom, right? Yes, I was sure I had.

Then I saw them. My sandals—size ten Reef Brazils on the floor just outside the girl's closet. With a sinking feeling, I realized that there was no way they could be mistaken for women's sandals. Why would a pair of guys' sandals be in her room? Maybe no one would notice, I prayed.

As I was waiting for someone to comment on my Reefs, the little brother went to take a piss. Good

> The author claims to have learned from this experience "that you should never assume parents will call to warn you that they are arriving early—and you should always flush your condoms."

call on the bathroom. Meanwhile, Mom, Dad, and Grandma were just chillin', and it looked like I might emerge unscathed.

Then suddenly the bed squeaked, and I felt severe pressure on my back as the air was pressed from my lungs. Apparently, Grandma had decided to sit on the bed. Outstanding. And I was still eyeing those sandals. They *had* to see them.

Gasping for breath and sensing an acute case of claustrophobia coming on, I was uncertain how much longer I could hold out. Finally, little brother was done with his business, and my gal had entered the bathroom to take a shower. At last, the rest of the family left the room.

I was still under the bed. In what seemed like an abnormally short period of time for a female to shower, the girl emerged from the bathroom.

"Hey, where are you?" she whispered. "Under the bed," I replied in a hushed tone. Her face appeared at ground level. "Hey, just stay where you are until we leave. Then my housemate will let you out," she said.

Much to my chagrin, I had to agree that this was probably the best plan under the circumstances. She put on clothes, and the sound of her footsteps on the stairs marked her exit. I heard muffled voices followed by the sound of the front door closing. Then silence. I wormed my way out from under the bed and put on my clothes. Cautiously, I made my way down the stairs. What if Mom forgot her purse and was on her way back to the front door?

The girl's housemate suddenly emerged from the kitchen, scaring the living crap out of me. She flashed an amused grin.

"Where did you hide?" she asked.

"Under the bed," I answered.

"Wow!"

And with that, I made my exit. I found out later that the girl's dad had asked her about the sandals. She made up some excuse that one of her guy friends had left them by the pool, and she was holding on to them for him.

Whether Dad bought that story or not I have no idea. Not that it matters. All's well that ends well—as long as I don't have to go crawling under a bed any time soon.

—*Baylor University*

Alumni Update: The author is currently attending law school at Baylor and "hating every day of it."

LESSON LEARNED: Prudence is taught to us one oh-shit-I'm-going-to-get-caught moment at a time. We know that hiding under a bed is a little clichéd, but the author showed terrific commitment and patience—which is admirable and understandable since a multigenerational ass-kicking was awaiting him.

Parents Versus the Party

During my sophomore year, I lived with my cousin Allison and her best friend, Shannon, both of whom were twenty-one. We lived in a nice off-campus, four-bedroom apartment that served as the gathering place for many parties. Shortly after that fall semester began, my housemates began planning a huge party in honor of my upcoming twentieth birthday.

The word "sophomore" means "wise fool" in Greek—making it an oxymoron, like "freezer burn" and "student athlete."

On the Thursday night two days before the party, my mom called and asked me what sort of plans I had for my birthday. I wasn't about to tell her the truth, because my parents were staunchly against alcohol and thought that I was a saint. So I told her that I was probably just going to study for a killer math test that I had the following Monday. I had good grades, and my parents assumed that I studied all the time. But then she said, "Well, forget studying. Your father and I are coming to visit you and take you out to dinner on Saturday night."

"Like hell you are," I was thinking. Of course, I didn't say that. What I said instead was, "But Mom, I really have to pass this test. Can't we do it some other time?"

Her response? "Oh, honey, you can study on Sunday."

Great!

I turned on the sweetness and begged them to come the next weekend, and eventually she agreed, much to my relief. I woke up on Saturday morning and met some of my friends to do a little tailgating before the 3:00 P.M. football game. After our victory, I was really pumped and definitely in a party mood.

Around 7:00 P.M., Allison decided that we didn't have enough beer. She insisted that I go with her to the liquor store, so we left Shannon by herself. On the way home, I decided to pull out the Jägermeister and start to work on it. A few minutes into the drive home, my cell phone rang. It was Shannon. My parents had just called and said they were in Austin and on their way to our apartment to surprise me. I almost dropped my phone (and the Jägermeister). We rushed back to the apartment so we could hide as much evidence as possible before the 'rents showed up.

Then the most bizarre and unimaginable thing happened. We stopped at an intersection. I was still chugging down the Jägermeister when I happened to look over at the vehicle next to ours. Staring back at me was my father, with my mother in the passenger seat! I quickly hid the liquor, but the look on my dad's face made it painfully clear that he had seen everything.

Think that's bad? It gets worse.

I called Shannon as soon as we pulled ahead of my parents and told her to hide the party shit and to make sure everyone knew to keep the hell away from our apartment.

> Parent-proof: Prepare a room for a visit from the parental units. This usually includes hiding alcohol, birth control devices, controlled substances, poor test grades, and dirty dishes.

We got home, with my parents right behind us. Then I noticed a very important detail that had somehow escaped me back at the intersection. My grandmother was with them. What the hell was my grandmother doing there?! "Oh, shit!" Allison muttered.

My parents gave both of us a stern look as they entered our apartment building. They had brought some food with them for us to keep at our place, and when we got upstairs they sent my grandmother to put the food in the kitchen. Then they pulled me into another room and lectured me on the evils of alcohol and launched into all kinds of whacked stories about when they were in college and how they knew what went on and how they were so disappointed in me. I wasn't paying much attention, however, as I was still thinking about what had happened back at the intersection and trying really hard not to crack up in front of them. I kept seeing the look on my dad's face when he turned and saw me with Mr. Jägermeister in hand. I mean, what were the odds?

Then things got worse. Someone knocked on the door, and my father went to open it. My grandmother was standing there looking rather uncomfortable. Then she spoke: "Sorry to interrupt, but some of this won't fit in the refrigerator—what with all the beer."

My dad turned to me, fuming. I closed my eyes and silently vowed to murder Shannon for being so stupid as to put the beer in the refrigerator. Needless to say, there wasn't much of a party that night.

My parents did make me go out to dinner with them, but they left soon afterward, both giving me a look of disapproval as they departed. I went back to our apartment and recounted the story for Allison and Shannon, and we all had a good laugh. We saved the liquor for the next weekend, and it was pure craziness. My story was a hit with everyone. I can't wait until the next birthday party.

—*University of Texas—Austin*

LESSON LEARNED: We hope everyone sees a pattern emerging: Parents can arrive at any time. And this will continue well past your college years. This is an important reason to always stay in touch with them. Sure, the bonding and the healthy adult relationship are nice, but what's most important is knowing when the hell they'll show up.

Meet the Parents

My freshman year of college, everything was exciting and new—including the fact that I learned to drink enough to impress even the seniors. As a college female, when you can outdrink fraternity boys, you know you're exceptional.

Unfortunately, this "talent" I had sometimes got me into some sticky situations. About a month or so into my second semester, my boyfriend asked me to go home with him to his parents' house for the weekend. I had gone home with him several times before, and I knew his parents loved me, so I agreed to go.

The first night there was fine. We all pretty much hung out and invited a few of my boyfriend's friends over—nothing too exciting. But the next night was very different . . .

> **Rents:** The people who raised you, helped pay for your schooling, and prompt wild cleaning sessions before they come to visit. Also called your Ps.

We went with his friends to a bar to hear a band, where we all proceeded to "tie one on." The beer and the shots were flowing, and we were all having a good old time. At the end of the night, my boyfriend and I went home to his parents' house and went to bed in his upstairs bedroom. (His parents were cool with that!) About two hours after passing out, I woke up and had to go to the bathroom. I was aware that I was still in a drunken stupor, so I was proud when I made it to the bathroom and back without falling or inflicting any other bodily harm upon myself.

> According to a 2005 National Sleep Foundation survey, 21 percent of adults report waking during the night because they have to go to the bathroom.

I crawled back into bed, cuddled up next to my boyfriend, and went back to sleep. I vaguely remember feeling someone next to me move, but I was too tired to respond. A few minutes later, the lights came on, and there were my boyfriend and his mom standing over me. My boyfriend was smirking, and his mom was try-ing not to laugh. Apparently, I hadn't gone to the right bedroom. Instead, I had crawled into bed between his mom and dad, and had cuddled up to his father! Needless to say, I didn't go visit them anytime soon after.

—Kent State University

LESSON LEARNED: Your other special talent should include the ability to out-drink frat guys, while also avoiding the undercover cuddle with their parents.

CHAPTER 8

School Daze 101

Teachers, Cheating, and Other Academic Misadventures

The Roman philosopher Cicero once noted, "The authority of those who teach is often an obstacle to those who want to learn." We'll take it a step further than ol' C-Dog and note that teacher authority is also an obstacle to those who want to skip class in favor of sleeping past noon, indulge in an early-afternoon power hour, or start the pre–football game tailgate a day or two early.

Lots of learning goes on in a college classroom, but sometimes it's not of an academic nature. Take the tale of a student who finds himself in the wrong class. While some may see this as a classical (albeit amusing) exercise in humiliation, we see it as an example of the power of laughter to transcend cultural and linguistic barriers. Want more? You'll also find stories herein of perseverance, patience, and ethics (cheating).

A word about cheating: It ain't cool, and if you're going to walk that line, you best know where "bending the rules" ends and "cheating" begins. Otherwise, be prepared to pay the consequences, or else have the guilt tear away at your stomach worse than a bottle of Lightning Creek MD 20/20.

While you probably won't find the answers to life's questions in a blue book, you may find some within the pages of this chapter.

Pardon, Frenchy?

I have a simple rule in life: if I can avoid being embarrassed in any way, I'll try my damnedest to do so. One of the most embarrassing scenarios that can occur in college, in my opinion, is when you walk into a class on the first day and sit down, and then, the professor walks in and says the name of the class, and—you're in the wrong class! In such a situation, you're forced to either "wait it out" and hope no one notices, or sheepishly gather up your belongings and walk out the door in front of everyone.

This happened to me on a couple of occasions. The first time, I felt so awkward that I stayed in the class for the entire time . . . *and took notes.* The second time it happened is why I'm writing this.

It was the first week of spring semester, and I needed to register for one more class. A friend of mine suggested French 240W because it was supposed to be an easy A, and because it was a "W" class, of which you needed three to graduate.

"Do you need to speak French?" I asked him. "No," he assured me. "It's a French history class."

Cool. I called up and registered. The first time I attended the class was actually its second meeting.

I sat down, and everyone was as friendly as could be. I even knew a

> **TOP FIVE FOREIGN LANGUAGE ENROLLMENTS IN U.S. INSTITUTIONS OF HIGHER EDUCATION**
>
> 1. Spanish
> 2. French
> 3. German
> 4. Italian
> 5. American Sign Language

girl in there. So, I figured everything was great. As soon as the professor walked in, though, a girl asked her a question in *perfectly spoken French.*

The professor then responded to the student in *perfectly spoken French.* I quickly started to panic. The teacher then looked at me and realized that I hadn't been there for the first class. I had a sinking feeling I was in big trouble, which was confirmed when she came toward me and said something to me . . . you guessed it, in French.

So, idiot that I was, did I calmly explain the situation? No. Instead, I looked at her, put on my best French accent, and said, "Pardon?"

> "Je suis dans la classe fausse" translates to "I'm in the wrong class."

So, she repeated what she had just said, still in French—and this is where this story took a turn for the worse. You see, I was extremely nervous, and when I get nervous, I start to laugh. So I started to laugh. But it came out like "Hunh HUNH!" My phony French laugh made me sound like a giddy Cajun. My ill-advised game of deception was over. So I sucked it up, gathered my belongings, and walked out.

A smooth exit made without drawing any attention to myself? Not quite. The laughter I heard from the room as I walked down the hallway was deafening.

—*University of Connecticut*

LESSON LEARNED: Love and laughter may translate well, but lying doesn't. A corollary is that if your bullshitting skills are lacking to begin with, they're likely to become exponentially worse when you're speaking a foreign language.

Professor Pain-in-the-Ass-and-Foot

During my sophomore year, I was required to take a class for my major from a professor I dreaded. He was one of those professors who double-tweak the grading scale so that it's nearly impossible to get a decent grade.

In a previous class with said professor, I had gotten what everyone else in the free world would have considered a B but which he dubbed a C+. So you can imagine how much fun I was looking forward to in my new class with him. I was determined to get an A even if it killed me. I went to every class, studied my butt off, and maintained a strong A during the first part of the semester.

Then I had to have surgery on my foot. I was able to give all of my professors a two-week warning about the surgery, and everyone was very understanding about it except my special professor.

He was also one of those professors who took attendance, and he reminded me that missing class would hurt my grade. He also informed me that a midterm I could not miss would be given a mere two days after my surgery.

I was willing to take the challenge. I had been to his class every day and taken notes like a maniac. If he was going to be this merciless, I could take it.

I had foot surgery on Monday. I was on heavy medication—Percocet, I believe—yet I made it to my appointment with my professor on Tuesday so I could get my notes from the class I had missed.

He handed me the notes and said, "You know, I should have had my secretary type these up since I can't even read them." Well, thanks! I studied them as well as I could but thought, "How much of this could possibly be on this test since it was only one day?"

Well, it was the whole test. The class was about how to write history, and this particular lecture had focused on mythology. The whole test referred to myths that were nowhere in the notes, and I had no clue.

I did the best I could and waited for my grade.

I received a D–. I was livid. I spoke to my professor after class and explained to him that I had done everything he had asked me to and that I was heavily medicated while I was taking the test.

He said, "Well, I don't know what more to say. Maybe if my TA had noticed that there was something wrong, I could do something about it." I flipped to the last page of my test, where the TA had written in red ink, "What is wrong with you? Your thoughts are scattered and do not make sense. Are you heavily medicated?"

At that point my professor could no longer argue with me, and he graciously (in his opinion) offered me the chance to combine my final grade with my midterm grade for an average final midterm grade. He was afraid that if I took the test over I would cheat, even though I assured him that I had no memory of having taken the test. *Grrrr.*

A few years later, I was up on campus chatting with a friend, and I noticed a man limping up the hill.

> Resident medical expert Dr. Brian Whirrett weighs in: "I'm no Sanjay Gupta, but in my opinion, the author of this story is fairly accurate in her account of what might happen if an 'inexperienced' opioid user took Percocet before a test. I'm amazed that this particular person actually stayed awake for the test, and that their ink was not smeared by drool stains."

Lo and behold, it was my professor dragging his recently operated-on foot along. I could not help but snicker.

Apparently there is a little bit of justice in this world.

—*Brigham Young University*

Alumni Update: The author moved on, graduated, got married, had a couple more foot surgeries, and now has a cute little family out west. Final thoughts? "Professors are people too, and they can be just as big jerks as anyone else." Ouch.

LESSON LEARNED: When dealing with academic types, remember that they lack the reality gland and are unable to excrete the empathy others can. To many a professor, the world ends at the threshold to their classrooms.

To Catch a Cheat

One would assume that cheaters employ more sophisticated means by the time they reach university, but that isn't always the case. During my third year, I had the misfortune of taking an intensely difficult trigonometry class. Dr. Kruger was notorious for failing 50 percent of his class every semester. At the end of every week he gave us a test. None was worth more than 5 percent, but like the pressure of passing, those tests added up.

One day, toward the end of the semester, I was settling down in my seat to take the weekly test. Halfway through the first question, it occurred to me that I had forgotten my calculator. This wasn't good. With a calculator I had at best a fifty-fifty chance of passing. Without one, I didn't have a prayer. Hoping to borrow one from a classmate, I tapped the shoulder of the boy sitting in front of me. The moment I laid my finger on his shoulder, he slumped down in his seat and collapsed to the floor.

I was shocked. There he was, lying before me, completely motionless. In a worst-case scenario, he was probably dead. In a best-case scenario, he had probably just passed out. I looked to the invigilators to see if they had noticed. They hadn't. I looked to the rows beside and in front of me to see if the other students had noticed. They hadn't. They were too absorbed in the test even to look up. Then I looked to the passed-out guy's desk. Sitting atop his test paper was a calculator—a real beauty, too, with two lines of scrolling text, graphing capabilities, and a nifty keyboard. He clearly wasn't using it, and I was sure to fail without it. Should I take it and risk going to Hell, or leave it and risk failing? This was a moral dilemma worthy of an Ethics class, not Trigonometry.

Looking around one last time to see if anyone had noticed the guy's lifeless body in the aisle, I reached down and snatched his hardware. My parents would know for certain if I failed Trig, but they would probably be long gone before finding out I had been assigned to Hell. To my relief, an invigilator noticed the guy. Granted, it took five minutes; I rationalized that many people have been revived after being dead for up to a half hour. There was a fair bit of commotion in the aisles. I feigned shock as people murmured and stared at the guy's body. Ten minutes later, paramedics were on the scene transporting him to the ER. On the bright side, it looked as though I was the proud owner of a fancy new calculator, a small price to pay for a terribly guilty conscience.

It wasn't until the next class that I recalled I still had the guy's calculator in my bag. Noticing he still wasn't present (a funeral, especially your own, is a pretty good excuse for missing class), I went to the professor and told him I had found something that I thought belonged to the student who had been rushed out of class. The professor gave me a wry smile and told me to keep it, telling me in the strictest confidence that the paramedics had discovered that the boy was merely faking a coma in order to get out of taking the test. As a matter of fact, they had discovered it the moment they carted him off and tried to revive him.

I instantly felt better. I may have been a slimebag, but at least my indiscretion had been a fairly private one.

To this day I'm not sure what's

> **HOW TO TELL IF SOMEONE IS TRULY UNCONSCIOUS**
>
> 1. Lay the person on his back.
> 2. Hold his "limp" hand one foot directly over his face.
> 3. Release the hand, letting it fall.
> 4. A truly unconscious person will smack himself directly in the nose.
>
> —Dr. Brian Whirrett, MD

worse, getting caught faking your own death or being powerless to stop someone from stealing your calculator while you're doing it. I've thought about tracking down the student to ask him, but I'm afraid he'd play dead if I tried.

—*McGill University*

Alumni Update: "I still have the calculator (as well as the lingering guilt for stealing it). I'm not certain what the coma faker is up to, but I'd like to think he's still routinely staging his own death to get out of performing mundane chores like taking out the trash, picking up the kids at soccer, and filing down his wife's corns. Whatever he's doing, I can guarantee you he's doing it without his calculator." —*Ryan Murphy*

LESSON LEARNED: You can't fake a coma. If you feel compelled to cheat, plan it out and do it right. And remember, if you try the old pretend-to-die trick, then prepare to get busted, embarrassed, and have your shit stolen.

Professorial Inspiration

One of the cool things about the University of New Hampshire when I went there was that you could take a lot of courses in Canadian studies. So I did, because I figured this meant a lot of field trips to Quebec: land of the eighteen-year-old drinking age and 3:00 A.M. last call.

So I ended up kind of a Canadian Studies groupie. I took all sorts of courses on the Great White North. As it turns out, they tricked me. They lured me in with promises of abundant Labatt's and then kept me because, sonofagun . . . the course work was *interesting.*

One of the guys who made it so fascinating was a fellow named Bob LeBlanc. Dr. LeBlanc taught several courses in Canadian geography. Not just physical geography—the Canadian shield, the St. Lawrence River, and all that—but human geography: long-lost settlements and Anglo-French immigration. Okay, that may or may not sound cool to you, but LeBlanc made it cool. He could take settlement patterns in a small eighteenth-century town in Quebec and reveal them as a microcosm of all North American history before the industrial revolution. And he'd do it in a quiet, good-natured manner. And you'd sit there riveted. Honest to god.

During my senior year, Dr. LeBlanc took us on a field trip to Montreal, which was to be a huge chunk of our grade. If you missed the field trip, you couldn't pass the class.

Yeah. You guessed it. I overslept. I woke up at eight thirty, threw some clothes on, and raced to the bus . . . and beheld an empty parking lot. So that was it. They were halfway to Vermont by now, and I'd just flunked the class.

Dejected, I slouched back to the dorm. Around lunchtime, two buddies stopped by to try to cheer me up. They were headed into Boston and said I should come along. It'd be fun, and it would take my mind off flunking the class.

That's when it hit me.

"Boston, huh? I don't suppose you'd mind dropping me in *East* Boston?"

The only thing in East Boston is Logan Airport, folks.

I hit the ticket counter at Air Canada at 1:00 P.M. . . . but there were no more flights to Montreal that day.

I figured that was it, but a kid at the ticket counter gave me the name of a pilot over at the cargo terminal. Sure enough, he was flying to Montreal that afternoon, and for fifty dollars he let me sit up front with him. (It was a more innocent time . . .)

Three hours later, I was landing at the Montreal airport. My taxi dropped me off at the hostel just as the bus with my class in it was pulling up!

I confidently joined the line of students as Dr. LeBlanc passed out a Xeroxed study sheet. When he came to me, he did a double take, then burst out laughing. He was flattered I had gone to such lengths for his class. Later, he bought me a beer and a small maple leaf pin to commemorate my journey. During dinner he told us about his adventures in places as diverse as Paris and Woonsocket . . . and the people he'd met and the things he'd learned from observing different people and cultures.

The rest of the field trip was informative and went smoothly. And yes, I passed the class.

In the years after that, I exchanged the occasional Christmas card with Dr. LeBlanc and thought about him whenever I swept a Canadian category on *Jeopardy*. He became professor emeritus of geography at UNH, and was well liked on campus. His position enabled him to travel the world attending geography conferences. In fact, that's where he was headed the morning of September 11. He was on board United Flight 175, bound for Los Angeles.

I don't really know why I chose to tell this story tonight. I occasionally reach back into the gray matter for some funny or outrageous anecdote

The late Dr. LeBlanc.

as a way to wind down after work or jog the writer's block. But tonight I settled on the story of my brief experience with Dr. Robert LeBlanc.

What happened on September 11 hit us all hard, and sometimes the enormity of it is still difficult for me to get my head around even a few years later.

But this isn't about terrorism, or national security, or the challenging state of the world, or the perplexing issue of where we go from here. This is a 9/11 story about a simple, crazy thing that happened in college, and how I got to know one of my professors better because of it, and how a nice guy touched my life in a small way. I'm sure he did the same for many others. So many people were lost on that day, they sometimes seem to disappear into sheer numbers. Bob LeBlanc was one of them. That's how I remember him—as a decent guy who loved what he did.

I just wanted to put a face to one of the numbers.

So, Professor, wherever you are . . .

Thanks.

—*University of New Hampshire*

Alumni Update: The Robert G. LeBlanc Memorial Fund was established at the University of New Hampshire Foundation through the generosity of the friends and family of Dr. LeBlanc. The fund's purpose is to provide financial assistance for University of New Hampshire undergraduate students to participate in international study. Donations may be made to the Robert G. LeBlanc Memorial Fund, c/o The UNH Foundation, 9 Edgewood Road, Durham, NH 03824.

LESSON LEARNED: Live for today. It's a recurring theme that we've illustrated in various lighthearted ways. We wanted to include this story to give some perspective and to underscore the importance of enjoying every minute of life.

CHAPTER 9

F——— the Police

Cops, College Students, and Other Legal Questions

It seems inevitable. Take a group of young, impressionable students with visions of rebellion dancing in their heads, mix in raucous parties and clouded judgment, and a meeting with the police will be just around the corner. And often, the results are about as pretty as a Mitch "Blood" Green street brawl with "Iron Mike" Tyson.

As badges are flashed and the threat of arrest becomes imminent, lessons are occasionally learned. For starters, there's the sinking realization that the difference between dealing with campus security and dealing with "real police" is akin to that between Chief Wiggum and Dirty Harry.

Second, although a jail cell may seem at a cursory glance to resemble the typical dorm room—constructed of cinder blocks, oozing with stink, and inhabited by a scary person in the bottom bunk—there's no safety net of campus to save you from cold, hard, permanent record–scarring reality. It's a lesson that some students have learned the hard way, sitting in jail with plenty of time to wrestle with inmates and nurse a hangover.

Do the crime and do the time. We hope you enjoy these stories of collegiate justice meted out, sometimes warranted, sometimes not.

The Not-So-Best Arrest

I always thought I'd get arrested for something, you know, *worthwhile*.

I was playing guitar when the police came to my dorm room. My friends and my roommate all left when the police asked them to. Alone in the room with them, I played a D chord over and over again on the guitar.

"Do you know why we're here?" the woman cop asked as the fat guy cop with the white mustache pulled every empty liquor bottle out of my closet. "Nope," I said. "Unless you've found the bumper to my car that got stolen two months ago."

"We're not here for that. Would you like to tell us what happened today?" she asked as that D chord went down a step.

What heinous crime had I committed? I started going over all the possibilities, and then settled on my having dropped my old television down four flights of stairs to the basement.

"You know, around . . . five o'clock," she said as Merle Haggard hoisted his belt and picked up my friend's fake ID from my desk and put it in his pocket.

The TV thing had happened only about two hours ago, so what the hell were they talking about? I switched to C, then to G, then back to D just to see what would happen.

"You'd better put down that guitar, young man," the lady cop said.

I played another chord.

Standing over me where I was half sitting, half lying on my beanbag chair, she reached into her front shirt pocket and pulled out a little white card.

"You have the right to remain silent," she read off of it.

If this had been a cartoon, you'd have seen my Adam's apple jump in my throat and would've heard a guitar string get tweaked up real high, as if it were going to snap. "Booooooyyiiiiiiiiiing."

The story's author adds, "The police didn't know how to put the handcuffs on right, and I had bruises on my wrists for days. (She put them on upside down.)"

"Whoa, whoa, whoa, what's this about?" I said as Hefty pulled me up by my armpits and turned me around so the woman cop could put the cuffs on me. "You want to tell us what happened at the Laptop Café?" she said, spinning me around.

I realized they were talking about the small campus dining hall by the journalism buildings. "Umm . . . no," I said. "Look, if this is about the television . . ."

"It's not about any television, young man. Although we do have you on video . . ."

"On video doing *what*?" I said as Pokey nudged a Beast Ice box out from under my bed with his foot.

"Not swiping your card at the dining hall," the woman replied.

Jesus Christ. Remembering now that I'd bypassed the line at the dining hall and just sat at a booth to enjoy my two bags of chips and iced tea, I realized I'd never gone back and swiped my card.

"It's a misunderstanding," I started to say, but the woman was wagging her finger at me like a schoolteacher. Her hair was up in some kind of professional bun, her cop suit all clean and starched. Who was she, anyway, having to read the Miranda rights off an index card?

"We have to make an example," she said. Bubba laughed, and I smelled stale coffee.

The courtroom smelled like roach killer and bat shit. The judge looked down at me and told me she had to work at eight the next morning, so I'd better not keep her up with this. She asked me why I'd done it, and warned me not to lie. I said it was a mistake. I told her I wouldn't do it again, and she said she knew that, and now everyone would know not to do it.

Just when I thought the situation couldn't possibly get any more ridiculous, she asked me to give her one good reason not to throw me in jail for the weekend. I told her that I had a final on Monday (true), and I hadn't studied for it (definitely true).

"Well, this is the only time in your life you'll ever be glad you have a final," she said, and smacked that circular thing on her desk with her wooden hammer. Considering the circumstances, I expected to see dust fly out that would date back to the eighteenth century.

If anyone asks, I just tell them I've never been arrested. The whole thing cost me a ten-dollar fine and fifteen hours of community service, which I never even did. Truth is, I'm afraid even to bring it up. I've got

> Judge Chamberlain Haller: "I don't like your attitude."
> Vinny Gambini: "So what else is new?"
>
> —from *My Cousin Vinny*

a feeling my picture is still in the police file cabinets, and my file is still open.

—*SUNY—Morrisville College*

LESSON LEARNED: The justice system don't work none. And to think that the cops and that judge wasted their time on that minor infraction when there are still heinous crimes committed every day on campus—like the use of contraband hot pots.

The Nazi Cops

I was attending a big party off campus, and they had this vodka-spiked watermelon. I ate several pieces; you really couldn't taste the vodka at all. Of course, after the watermelon and some brews, I was trashed. Eventually, I swiped a twelve-pack and headed out.

I staggered down the street chugging a beer. I've always had a shitty sense of direction, and when I'm drunk it's almost nonexistent. As I walked along, I was feeling angry and frustrated, and it didn't help that I had no idea where I was going. Soon, I was hopelessly lost.

At one of the more ramshackle houses, there were some long-haired rednecks out on their front porch. They looked friendly enough, so I figured I'd ask them for directions. But in my drunken state, I chose an ill-advised greeting: "Hey, you guys got any reefer?"

> According to Emily Post, acceptable informal greetings include " 'Good morning' and on occasions 'How are you?' or 'Good evening.' " "Got any reefer?" is not mentioned.

The men just sat there, expressionless, but the fat woman with them jumped up and screamed at me hysterically, "No! Get out of here, you drunk!"

Undeterred, I set the twelve-pack and my open beer down beside the steps and said, "Who the hell you guys think you're fooling? I can just look at you, with your long hair and shit, and tell you've got some reefer. Now fire up a doobie!"

The guy with the beard stood up. "Fuck off, asshole. Get out of here or I'll kick your ass."

My philosophy was always to strike first, so I jumped the guy, got him in a headlock, and wrenched him to the ground. We rolled around in the grass for a while, when suddenly the yard was bathed in blue light. Cops. We jumped up and tried to act like nothing had happened. But the others were screaming at the cop to arrest me even before he got out of his car.

"Shut up!" the cop told them. Then, taking me aside, he asked me what was going on. "Well, Officer, I was just walking down the street minding my own business when these people called me a sissy college boy and a fag. I know I should have just ignored them, but they kept taunting me. So I replied in kind."

"You mean you called them fags, too?" he asked.

"No sir," I replied. "I called them rednecks."

"You haven't by any chance been drinking, have you, boy?" he asked.

"Uh, two beers," I lied. "About an hour ago." I had already anticipated the second part of the question, having learned from experience. "Perhaps the beer impaired my judgment," I added. "Usually I would have just walked away from such provocation." I was starting to lay it on a bit thick, but luckily the cop swallowed my bull and approached the rednecks.

After a short discussion with them, during which they ranted and raved, the cop returned to where I was standing and said, "They claim that you approached them and demanded drugs."

"Well, sir, I really didn't want to mention it, because I didn't want to get them in trouble. But that's what started the whole thing. They tried to sell me marijuana." Boy, was I on a roll.

"Where do you live?" the cop asked.

"Over on Aylsford Avenue," I replied.

"Well, you run on home now," he said. "I'll take care of these people."

Just when I was on the brink of escaping from this predicament, I made a major misstep. "Uh, just one thing," I said to the cop. "Could you point me in the right direction?"

"What?!"

"I've become a little bit disoriented by this whole ordeal," I said. "Could you just give me directions back to my house?" The cop grabbed my arm, whipped me around, and slammed me against the hood of his car, then slapped the cuffs on me. All very smoothly and professionally; he was definitely good at his job.

Some twenty minutes later, I was in a grimy cell with about thirty other prisoners. The walls were painted piss yellow and peppered with graffiti.

The toilet was a metal job without a seat filled almost to overflowing with toilet paper and feces, and the stench filled the cell.

Two of the walls were lined with benches, but all the seats were taken. Plenty of people were standing: Nobody dared sit on the nasty floor. I was exhausted and wanted to rest, and I still had a strong mean streak running through me. One guy was stretched out with his feet up on the bench, taking up more than his share of space. I grabbed his feet and slung them violently off the bench, and then plopped myself down.

Without hesitation, the guy smacked me good across the face—not a punch, but an open-handed smack. I jumped him and got him in a head-lock, wrestling him to the floor. It was the same scenario as earlier, only instead of grass, I was rolling around on a filthy jail floor.

I had gained the upper hand when three cops came in and broke up the fight. They threatened to throw everyone in the cell into the drunk tank if we didn't settle down. I didn't see how the drunk tank could be much worse than the cell we were in, but the others assured me that it was.

Soon after that, another cop came and got me. I was fingerprinted and led to a small room where I was commanded to strip down. A shriveled old bum was in there with me, his skin yellow and wrinkled. "I'm glad you taught that asshole a lesson," the bum said, as we stood there naked. "I hate his goddamn guts."

"Yeah, well, he deserved it," I said.

To kill time while I hung out naked, I went up to the counter and looked around. A comic book lay out on the counter. It was titled *Helga: The Girl Who Loved the S.S.*, and there were swastikas all over the damn thing. Helga was a buxom blond babe: on the cover she was shown leading a parade of Nazis, holding aloft a Nazi flag. I picked the book up and thumbed through it. I'd never seen anything so fucked up in my life. In fact, the only way I could take it was as some sort of a joke. So I laughed my ass off. "Where the hell did you get this?" I asked the cop behind the counter.

"Oh, it's from our library," the cop said. He was laughing, too.

"You must have one hell of a library."

"You'd better believe it."

But once I considered the matter, I began to wonder: Why had they set the book there, in plain view of everyone who came through? To intimidate Jews and minorities? Perhaps that was just their ordinary reading material and they didn't think anything of it, didn't imagine anyone could find it offensive, or else they simply didn't care.

Next we were all moved to the overnight lockup, a large room with rows of bunk beds. Since I was one of the first in the door, I managed to get a top bunk. I was worried that the guy I had fought would come and slit my throat as I slept. In fact, I worried that I wouldn't be able to sleep at all. But I needn't have been concerned; I was so drunk that I went out like a light, facedown on the cold steel bed.

I awoke before dawn. Nobody had slit my throat, I noticed with some relief. I saw a cop walking by and went up to the bars.

"I have to be in class at nine this morning," I said.

"Bah, ha, ha!" the cop burst out laughing. "It's Saturday, you idiot!"

"Yes sir, I know. I have a class on Saturdays."

"Bah, ha, ha! You lying sack of shit!" he said as he walked away.

They didn't let me out until that evening. That longest day of my life was spent battling monotony, boredom, and depression . . . and I'll never forget that nasty hangover or the goddamn Nazi book.

—*University of Kentucky*

Alumni Update: "At least I've managed to stay out of jail since then and even graduated from college. These days, I live in the Chelsea Hotel in New York City. You can read my tales of life at the Chelsea in my weekly 'Slice of Life' column at legends.typepad.com, the Hotel Chelsea blog."

LESSON LEARNED: Know how to throw down a sweet headlock. This is an advanced track of study for anyone who plans to go from fun-loving student to head prisoner just hours away from buying a shiv for a carton of cigs.

Mugging for the Camera

We were bored. And when we get bored, we get inventive.

I was outside of my dorm smoking with three friends and staring into the lobby at the TV. As always, it was displaying the live footage from the surveillance camera in the basement. All you ever saw on that damn screen was the empty hallway and the door. Never was there a soul on the screen.

We decided to change that.

Amy and I went down to my room, leaving our two friends to watch the TV from outside. Amy put on a hooded rain parka and pulled the drawstring until only a tiny portion of her face was showing. Then she unscrewed a pool stick so it was only half size. I grabbed my purse.

I walked into the hallway that the camera was covering. I pretended to talk on a cell phone in the little corridor while Amy sneaked up on me from behind. She "struck" me on the back with the pool stick, and I collapsed to the ground. She kept savagely "beating" me with the pool stick and kicking me. Our choreography was fabulous, mostly because she would talk me through it: "I am approaching you, now hitting your left shoulder, kicking you, kicking you, one more kick for good measure." She then wrestled my purse from me, beat me with it a few times, and left me "for dead" on the floor.

Our friends immediately called and made us do it again. Please realize that the TV that broadcasted our exploits was the first thing anyone who entered the building would see. Of course, we agreed to a repeat performance. In the course of the evening, I think I was "mugged" eight times. The last time we did it, we added a new scene. After I was beaten with the pool stick, kicked, robbed, and beaten with my own purse, I was then run over by a large blue cart.

After we pulled the cart off of me, Amy and I rejoined our audience upstairs in the lobby. Just then, we

> Have a running list of the really dumb things you did in college. That way, when you screw up as an adult you can say, "Well, it could be worse. I could be stranded in a pool of my own piss on the Sigma Chi hall."
>
> —Ashlyn Broderick

heard the sirens. A USCPD [University of South Carolina Police Department] car zoomed up to the front of our dorm. Let me just say, I was getting a little nervous.

A cop jumped out, opened his trunk, and grabbed an axe. He then raced into the building and straight to the elevator. Okay, I was about to shit my pants. My bowels must have had superhuman strength, though, because even as two more USCPD cars screeched to a halt in front of our building, I did not shed one drop of bodily fluid. (I checked later.) We were really curious, at the time, to know why the cop was carrying an axe. I mean, Amy was hostile in the video, but surely that warranted a gun more than this gigantic cleaver, right?

Amy and I were trying to be calm, while fully realizing that we were complete morons. C'mon, faking assault and battery—what the fuck were we thinking? Amy was seriously getting more than a little freaked out as she realized that she was still wearing the assailant's rain parka and brandishing the deadly weapon (aka the pool cue).

Then, by some instance of fate, second chances, or just sheer luck, the two police cars sped away to the dorm beside ours. The cop with the axe came back to the lobby and ran out of the building, hopped in his car, and sped down to the next dorm as well. Amy and I were stunned. Apparently a freshman had attempted suicide in the dorm next door, and the ingenious USCPD had come to our dorm by mistake.

A steady stream of nicotine helped us calm our rattled nerves and come to our senses. That night, we learned an important lesson: surveillance cameras are there for a reason—to keep me entertained!

—*University of South Carolina*

Alumni Update: "Now I'm actually a federal investigator, making sure people like me come nowhere close to obtaining federal employment."

LESSON LEARNED: The system sometimes demands a checkup. Every now and then during this long car trip called life you need to reach across the seat and poke at authority. Carry a security tag close to the shoplifting sensors, pull the fire alarm, and re-create a mugging—all in the name of keeping the man on his toes.

CHAPTER 10

System of a Clown

A History of Revolution
and Battling the Administration

"The time has come for someone to put his foot down," says Dean Vernon Wormer in *Animal House*. "And that foot is me." That sentiment, so eloquently stated, is pretty much the norm when it comes to school administration philosophy across the country.

If you're a college student, what to do with all these rules and regulations keeping you down? Fight the power, of course. And what better way to do so than by formulating a wicked scam sure to win you the admiration of your peers while striking a blow to the dastardly school administration? (Extra points for getting on the evening news.)

Of course, every hero needs an enemy. That's why we view the administration as a worthy adversary for some good old-fashioned butting of heads, rather than as a truly evil monster. And as an added benefit to this rabble-rousing, the lessons learned in circumventing the system come in handy for ensuring your survival in the real-world business hierarchy—not to mention for stopping a big developer from destroying the neighborhood recreation center.

Enjoy these tales of spirited rebellion—or, as Melvin and Mario Van Peebles put it, "How to Get the Man's Foot Outta Your Ass."

Our Lady of Shameless Scams

I had been on campus for only three beer-fueled days when my room-mate, Teddy, and I were accosted by a bright-faced coed who stopped us dead in our tracks. It was 8:00 A.M. We were on our way home from an all-night bender while this girl was clearly just starting her day. "Welcome to McGill from Smile McGill," she announced in a sing-songy voice.

As it turned out, Smile McGill was a collection of over-caffeinated students that served as a welcome wagon during the first two weeks of orientation. Frankly we were amazed that anyone would want to be part of such an organization, but what was even more amazing was that Smile McGill was an officially sanctioned club with office space, free long-distance and faxing privileges, and a budget! Inveterate scammers, Teddy and I recognized a golden opportunity. All we had to do was make up our own bogus club and we, too, could be partying on the Students Society's tab.

Of course, all of the obvious clubs already existed: from sports and recreational clubs to movie-viewing groups. What we had to do was come up with a club they couldn't possibly refuse. We came up with a religion: Our Lady of the Epileptic Vision.

Creating your own religion, we found, is easier said than done. Just ask the members of Heaven's Gate. For starters, you have to create a doctrine and a creed, and most important, you have to come up with an explanation as to why no one has ever heard of you before.

According to the story we dreamed up over a plate of hot wings, the religion was founded in 1913 in Kansk, a town deep in the Siberian heartland, when a thirteen-year-old received a powerful vision during an epileptic fit. Unfortunately, religion in Russia was still seen as being "the opiate of the masses," so faith in Our Lady of the Epileptic Vision was kept on the down low in its native country. When Russians began immigrating to the United States, small pockets brought the religion with them, practicing it and spreading the message to others. But this was during the height of McCarthyism, so once more the religion took to base-

> Joseph McCarthy, who served as a U.S. senator from the state of Wisconsin from 1947 to 1957, was a notoriously heavy drinker.

Our Lady of the Epileptic Vision

We hold strongly the ethical quality of the universe made distinct by the all-encompassing glow of *The Bozhestvennaya* and combatted by the omnipresence of avarice, greed and acts of human defiance. We hold true the teachings of *The Chosen One* and are to act as to promote the holy tetrad of benevolence, tolerance, equality and spiritual devotion.

The 4 Principles of Devotion

1. Drug or alcohol consumption of any kind pollutes the purity and sanctity of the body and are against the teachings of *The Chosen One*.

2. Violence of any kind towards society or individuals (Human, Animal or Plant) disrupts the human mind, clouding it and causing it to veer from our intended course of pure existence.

3. We must respect other religions in order for the populous of our earth to become a true community. Respect for all races, cultures and genders must also deepen.

4. Religious truth is not absolute, but relative.

Creed of Devotion

All grace is due to *The Bozhestvennaya*, creator and sustainer of our cosmos, and I bear witness that there is none purer than she, and as children of the divine order of her design, we are her obedient devotees. May the pristine warmth of her peace and blessing cleanse the impure, depraved souls of all mankind. **Da Budet Tak.**

The very real documents from the very fake religion.

Our Lady of the Epileptic Vision
and
The McGill Society of Steadfast Christian Virgin

proudly present a night of knee-slapping revelry and madness as they present...
Not Between My Legs You Don't!

Friday Febuary 16, PLAYER's THEATRE $2 students $3 adults

ments and root cellars—remaining a secret to most. In fact, it wasn't until recent years, and in cities as tolerant as Montreal, when people felt free to express their faith in Our Lady of the Epileptic Vision.

All that remained was to find an obscure picture of a Russian-looking woman and slap it on a piece of paper. Two hours and fifty cents in photocopies later, we were done.

Our next step was to pitch our club to the Students Society. We made an appointment for the following week. In the meantime, we hung posters of our creed and mission statement all over campus. Most people had no clue what they were reading, but it created buzz and made us a known—albeit highly suspicious—commodity.

By the time we had our meeting, the five-person review board at the Students Society had heard of us and were willing to listen to our pitch. We told them about our principles, we talked about our history, and we even led them in a quick prayer session. In fact, we did everything but drop down to the ground and fake a seizure.

To our shock, they bought it. Granted, there was some skepticism when we explained why there was no documentation. But as true Canadians, they were more concerned with not offending us than with admitting a fraudulent religion into their university. Religious discrimination, we were discovering, could be a very powerful tool.

We were given our own office space in the student union building and put on temporary probation for one semester, a standard procedure for any new club.

On our first "Activities Night," most people weren't sure what to make of us, while others were grateful for something else to put on their résumés. By the end of the night we had signed up thirty students for our first meeting (an event that we kept on postponing to protect what little credibility we still had).

And so it was that Our Lady of the Epileptic Vision opened its doors for business. There were never any services, or any outings as we had promised, but the money came in and we kept that office space for two years. To this day, Teddy and I still hoist a beer every May 5 in honor of the Divine Feast of the Gesticulant Seizure. It should never have worked, but it did, and for that, we thank God . . . um, rather, the *Bozhestvennaya*.

—McGill University

Alumni Update: "Since leaving university, I went on to become a professional stand-up comedian, gracing some of the largest stages across North America as well as some stages that were just overturned tables in dimly lit Legion halls. My friend, meanwhile, is now putting elementary school kids through their paces as a Phys Ed teacher in Ontario. Neither one of us has created another cult since our college days, but if we get enough white robes and Nikes together, anything is possible."

LESSON LEARNED: Like a wise man on Ricki Lake once said, "Don't hate the player. Hate the game." (And how can you even hate the game?) These lovable reprobates show off both impressive thinking skills and impressive amounts of sacrilege.

Community Full Service

"There will be a pretty big fine," the judge said. "And fifty hours of community service."

As I stood next to my bald and tattered-clothed public defender, I knew he hadn't done a good job. The man looked more hungover than I did.

"But I don't have *any* money," I told the judge. "None."

Not looking amused, she told me, "Well, you'd better scrape some up. Your lawyer will give you a list of community service activities in your area. We hope you've learned your lesson."

I learned my lesson all right. Get a job so you never have to resort to a public defender.

Back in my room I looked over my community service sheet. Town of Nelson Food Pantry was the one highlighted. Why would my lawyer highlight that?

At the time, I was so broke that I was buying spaghetti and Cheez Whiz because it was cheaper than a box of macaroni and cheese. I was boiling chopped-up hot dogs in ramen noodles and adding oatmeal just so hunger wouldn't keep me awake.

In a survey in 2000, the citizens of Japan voted instant ramen noodles as the top Japanese invention of the twentieth century.

I took my cab ride to the food pantry. The lady at the desk told me I would be in charge of separating out all the stuff that they couldn't give to the homeless.

"Anything with alcohol goes in the bag," the lady said and handed me a giant burlap sack. "Any kind of medicine, mouthwash, hair gel. Sometimes you'll find whole bottles of liquor. Restaurants don't want to throw it out, so they give it to us. We can't give it to the homeless, though, so it gets thrown out. They can't have makeup, either, because it has poison in it, and they'll try to eat it. Nail polish has alcohol. You'll take all the stuff that can't be donated, and you'll drive it out to the dump."

"I don't have a car," I told her. "I take a cab."

"Then you take it in the trunk of the cab and throw it out at the dumpster on campus. I don't care what you do, but it doesn't stay here."

Just then I thought of my lawyer with his red boozer radish nose and his eyeglasses falling down his face, and I knew exactly what I was going to do. Needless to say, when I got back to the dorm, the burlap sack didn't go in any dumpster. I hauled it directly up to my fourth-floor room.

It was January in central New York State, and that means four solid months of colds and flus and strep throat. Within twenty minutes, I was auctioning off NyQuil for a buck a bottle.

Within an hour, I had my wares spread all over my dorm floor, with girls picking out their favorite hair spray and nail remover, guys snapping up codeine and ibuprofen, and those little sample liquor bottles from the restaurants selling for five dollars a pop.

> There's a sucker born every minute, but none of them ever die.
>
> —Con man known as "Paper Collar Joe," but falsely ascribed to P. T. Barnum.

In two weeks I wasn't taking a cab to the Town of Nelson Food Pantry. I had my own used car I'd bought through the want ads for three hundred dollars.

They loved me there. I worked *fast*. I wanted this community service to last all year. I knew exactly what people wanted, and I even started taking orders before I left.

"Mary Kay!" the sorority girls said.

"Calvin Klein cologne!" the frat guys demanded.

"I need some Benadryl," the sick ones told me. "Antibiotics, anything!"

"I just want the liquor!"

After my fifty hours were up, I had to go back to the courthouse and pay my fine. I could have paid it one hundred times over. I'd stopped eating ramen after my first day at the Town of Nelson Food Pantry and started taking my friends out to dinner.

In the courthouse, my lawyer coughed into a snot rag and asked for my record to be wiped clean because of the exemplary letters the people at the pantry had written about my diligence in making a difference and my commitment to working there.

If it weren't for him and his belief that college students can get out of anything if just given a nudge in the right direction, I don't know how I would have gotten through that semester.

I bought my first car and was able to pay the monthly insurance. I sold the car for more than I bought it for to some kid from out of state. I cured the sick and made even the homeliest girl look good for only a couple bucks' profit. I sold more liquor than the corner store and didn't ask for ID.

So even though I failed Economics, I think I knew the value of supply and demand. Oh, and of course being a service to the community.

—*SUNY—Morrisville College*

LESSON LEARNED: Be a card-carrying opportunist in life. When life—or the judge—hands you lemons, sell them on the black market as rare yellow limes, set up a smuggling ring, and start your own citrus empire.

Mascot Madness

As an undergrad at James Madison University, I was interested in pushing the boundaries of the academic experience. I applied to be a part of an innovative interdisciplinary arts class with a course description that invited students to "fuck shit up," or at least that's how I read it. The class was comprised of twenty wild-and-crazy students from the fields of Dance, Music, Visual Arts, Theater, and Video and Film Production. Despite the fact that I was a Sociology major with no verifiable art cred, they still let me in.

For my final project, I decided to orchestrate a media prank. I began by writing letters to the campus newspaper, making up absurd claims about why the JMU school mascot, the Duke Dog, should be replaced with a far superior creature.

Because it was the height of the

JMU's Duke Dog is a tribute to Samuel Page Duke, the university's second president.

PC movement backlash, I intentionally pushed buttons with lines like "It seems sexist to honor an aggressive, masculine dog wearing a crown—a symbol of historical patriarchal oppression." Soon, regional newspapers picked up on the story, helping to make a nonexistent movement a reality, or at least a demented simulacrum of said reality.

I collected more than four hundred signatures for a petition that favored changing the Duke Dog to "Dukie the Three-Eyed Pig with Antlers." This petition fueled the paranoia of those who feared my noble cause might prevail. At the height of the nuttiness, the front page of the paper listed the day's top news stories in order of importance: (1) "Duke Dog Controversy"; and (2) "Traumatic Drama at Gunpoint: Find Out How a JMU Grad Dealt with Being Shot."

A Student Government Association senator (and roommate of mine) submitted a bill in favor of changing the mascot. In response, a group of students started a petition to "Save the Duke Dog" and submitted a legislative proposal to prevent this semiotic coup from happening.

During that year's homecoming game, the marching band wrote WE LOVE THE DUKE DOG inside their tubas and wore plastic dog bones around their necks in a sign of solidarity. Fight the power. Down with the pigs. During the game someone threw an effigy of a three-eyed pig with antlers into the stands, and the crowd ripped it to shreds. One conversation overheard at the game: "Why are they ripping that stuffed animal to shreds?" "Some fags are trying to change the mascot to a three-eyed pig with antlers." "Oh."

What to do next? Well, a rally, of course, planned on Halloween 1991, my twenty-first birthday. To ensure a high profile for the event, I officiated a mass wedding ceremony, where I married about one hundred people to bananas. Yes, bananas. Two television stations showed up to cover the event, and the NBC story was broadcast on all NBC affiliates in the state of Virginia. The footage was incorporated into a CNN story about opposition to racially offensive mascots like the Washington Redskins and the Atlanta Braves. The funniest part about the original NBC broadcast is that no one noticed that our friend Greg, dressed in the Duke Dog outfit, started simulating masturbation behind the reporter.

Although quite a few people picked up on the fact that this was a joke, far more became quite angry, which made me the target of many harassing phone calls and a couple of instances of vandalism. (Someone stole my antlered pig lawn ornament, and when I got a replacement antlered pig, the new one was smashed to bits.)

After the rally and the ensuing television coverage, the largest regional paper, *The Roanoke Times & World News,* ran a front-page story on the whole affair. During an interview with the reporter, I decided to lie brazenly to see what they would print without fact-checking. I made up the existence of a Nancy X, a fictional woman who had supposedly invented Dukie, and casually explained that a pig with antlers was a pagan symbol of sexuality. "I mean, of course everybody knows that the three-eyed pig with antlers was a pagan symbol of sexuality," I remember telling the reporter.

Why did I go to all this trouble? I did get three credits toward my degree, but I mostly thought it would be funny to irritate and hoodwink people who had no sense of humor. The event can also be seen as a little social-psychology experiment. Substitute the American flag for the Duke Dog, and you can understand why quite a few people got mad when this icon was threatened by a three-eyed pig with antlers.

It was also a critique of mass media. First, news outlets gave broad coverage to a trivial event when there were plenty of politically explosive issues that were either downplayed or ignored. Second, media can, in effect, make something real that is a complete fabrication. Think about what I, a relatively unsophisticated college student with no money and a little free time on his hands, was able to do, and then compare it with the resources available to lobbying organizations and large corporations. They have millions of dollars at their disposal, which buys them far greater access than a twenty-one-year-old punk.

One final point—something that I think scarred me for the rest of my life: I only got a 98 for my final project. I mean, c'mon! What would it have taken for me to get those extra two points?

—James Madison University

Alumni Update: Kembrew McLeod is now a professor in the Department of Communication Studies at the University of Iowa. He has produced several documentaries and authored books on the topic of copyright. He also made news for trademarking the term "freedom of expression" and selling his soul on eBay. Oh, the places you'll go after a college prank.

LESSON LEARNED: While it might do them some good, most people don't like their paradigms shifted, not even jiggled a little—which is all the more reason to keep doing it.

Sisters in Charity Cheating

It seemed like a good idea at the time of registration. How tough could a class known as "Math for Morons" possibly be? The class seemed simple enough at first. Drag myself to a lecture with four hundred of my closest friends, sit there in a vegetative state, and take notes every now and then as I saw fit. But then came the catch—and there's always a catch.

Test time rolled around, and I saw that they planned to examine our remedial mathematic aptitude at 8:30 P.M. on a Friday. Great! My grade just dropped from an A to a C, because I accepted the reality that I would not be able to find the self-control to stay away from happy hour on Friday, in the fall, during football season. Score another one for the administration.

Semester over, lesson learned? Of course not.

Three semesters later, I found myself in a class called Exceptional People, which preached about accepting people of all backgrounds, lifestyles, handicaps, etc. The frighteningly high and ever-present potential for the auditorium to bust into rounds of "Kumbaya" was enough to induce vomiting, but come on, how hard could this class be?

> EEX 3312: Exceptional People in School and Society is offered by the University of Florida's College of Education and is worth three credits.

The lecture hall in which the course was held played host to about 650 students, so how many times would we actually have to go to class, right? Also, it was one of those courses that a small herd from each Greek house signed up for, so you're on the buddy system for anything that might require more than a pulse, or random attendance sign-in sheets—or so we thought.

Then—conveniently *after* the drop/add period was over—came the catch. A fleet of TAs came out of nowhere, and we were put into teams. Teams that checked their own attendance. Teams that checked their own homework. Teams that eliminated every way we thought we would get out of doing real work for this course. And the real clincher, the way the TAs truly earned themselves the title of TEAM NO FUN, was when they informed us that we would need twenty community service hours from a list of pre-approved organizations.

There it was: the wet blanket on our fire, the bad hair on our prom night, and the fumble on our one-yard line.

As I stood with one of my best friends, our immediate thoughts went to how we could stick it to the system and scam our way out of this. First we thought, "No problem! We're already required to do service for our sororities." That spark of genius was quickly extinguished as the TAs informed us that whatever service we did as our own extracurricular activities (e.g., all things sorority) did not count.

Still, where there's a will to slack off, there's often a way. Determined to B.S. our way out of the situation, we signed up for some kind of blind service–related thing. But after abandoning the project for another few weeks, we got that "oh shit" feeling that we really needed to get going on it, or the end result would not be favorable.

By this point, we were looking at having to do a sizable amount of service each week to complete the twenty hours. Then, to rub salt in the wound, we got word that our grade would go down proportionately to the amount of this crap we piled on at the end of the semester. That's when we knew it was all or nothing with the bullshitting skills, so we went to work.

The first step was to concoct a story. We stayed late one day in a post-class Team No Fun meeting and whined to our TA about how we'd been doing service for this great organization the whole time, in fact we'd done well over the twenty required hours, but wouldn't you know it, it wasn't one of the preselected organizations. We were just sick to our stomachs that we'd done everything wrong. We lied through our teeth and offered to pile all of the twenty hours into a couple of weeks for another organization, if they would forget about the time/grade ratio for us. Captain Personality told us that she would have to discuss it with our actual teacher, but she'd get back to us the next class period.

Kara and I once again apologized profusely and waited until we were forced back into this pointless class. The TA found us and informed us that, though they weren't supposed to, with proper documentation from the organization and the name of a contact person, they'd let us pass on the "service we'd been doing for the blind." The next step was to set up a voice mail service for the fictional blind lady we'd been driving around

Gainesville, as well as one for the fictional woman who'd been supervising us.

Easy enough. We headed straight to our past sorority president and vice president, and told them the debacle we'd gotten ourselves into. They told us we were morons, but commended our efforts and agreed to create voice mails for us that they would answer, should our TA call.

Then it was on to printing up stationery for the fake organization and getting fake signatures from all the completely fictional people who'd supervised us and who ran the project. How better to find a bunch of people with nothing to do than by going door to door in the sorority house? Some people found the idea morally unacceptable, so we promptly rolled our eyes at them, slammed their doors, and talked shit about them as we walked to the next room. Finally, we got it all done and handed in the projects.

Grades came out before the semester ended, and we found we had pulled it off beautifully. We both received As in the course for a job well done.

Some of you might be thinking, "Hey, they probably spent nearly twenty hours and a lot more money trying to get out of it." You might be right. Congrats, you're also a tool and missing the point.

The point is we didn't spend twenty hours of our lives doing something we had no interest in, and in the process we got some really great experience in triumphing over the less-than-desirable situations we all get ourselves into.

—*University of Florida*

Alumni Update: "I still manage to B.S. my way out of most of the crap I get myself into. Sometimes I wonder how I'm still holding down a job, or who would hire me in the first place. Then I realize how it all goes back to the ability to successfully execute B.S. Not only can it get you out of something (homework/attendance-based classes/tests), but applied in the real world, it can also get you into something (e.g., a job). All of us involved in this story are in the working world; I'm in New York working in media."

LESSON LEARNED: If you're going to blow off your community service, you might as well create an elaborate scam that allows you to hone your problem-solving skills, tenacity, and teamwork in the process.

DUMB SMARTIES

*I have never met a man so ignorant
that I couldn't learn something from him.*
—Galileo Galilei, Italian astronomer and physicist

While Galileo may have been right, some of our stories come close to proving him wrong. Despite all of the value placed on education and the praise lauded on graduates, students can really act like idiots. And we hope you agree that their idiocy makes for good readin'.

Maybe it's because everyone wants to see the elite falter. Maybe it's the irony in smart people doing dumb stuff. Or maybe it's just fun to see young adults behave so ridiculously—especially when you see the train wreck coming. (Check out the story about a hot pepper seed, a urethra, and an ill-advised dare—you know where that's going.)

Thankfully, the campus provides a safe environment for this type of behavior. The cops are rented, the furniture is industrial-strength, and the slaps on the wrist are few and far between. College serves as just one big buffer before the real world—setting the stage for four to six years rife with dumb-ass behavior.

And the lesson to be learned? It's best to catch a bad case of the stupids before you can do any real damage in the real world. The following chapters prove that the nation's best and brightest are quite often neither.

CHAPTER 11

And We Could've Gotten Away with It

Analysis of the Botched Scheme

The best-laid plans of mice and men often go awry. This is particularly true if the mice are freshmen and the plans involve something they really shouldn't be doing. Welcome to the wonderfully demented world of botched schemes—attempts to pull something off that go way, way wrong—which hold a special place in our hearts.

These stories offer a unique insight into students' decision-making process—or lack thereof. The real beauty of the botched scheme is that it underscores a big difference between students and normal people. Where a normal person would admire a well-manicured lawn, a student would try to figure out how to steal the lawn gnome and use it to scare his roommate Barry shitless. And that's just for beginners.

The ultimate benefit of these tales of tragic blunders is that they teach us—and our mischievous protagonists—the value of going from vision ("We should steal that picture!") to execution ("Here is a reasonable way to steal that picture!").

So here is a salute to the plans that have gone awry, because without them, plans B and C would never see the light of day.

The Chipper Stripper

For my friend Allie's nineteenth birthday, we really wanted to surprise her with a stripper. Neither my friends nor I had any money to spend. So, knowing that there were plenty of horny undergraduate males willing to get naked at the drop of a hat, we planned a scheme: We made signs asking if a guy would be willing to do a striptease for our party. We made it clear that the guy would be doing it just for the thrill of it. We put the signs up in all the boys' bathrooms in our dorm.

The only person to come through ended up being a friend of a friend. He was totally psyched to strip; he even recorded his own mixed CD for the occasion. When the time came, we handed the stripper Allie's birthday cake and he danced on into our dorm room, which was packed with girls, wearing tear-away pants and a wife beater. He set the cake down, tore off his pants and ripped off his top, revealing some shiny, silky boxers. As the lap dance progressed, the boxers came off and he was wearing only a leopard-print man thong.

We could tell that he was starting to really get into the act—if you know what I mean. His turgid package was being thrust very close to Allie's face. She started laughing, half out of embarrassment and half out of disgust. Just as he was coming forward with one of his thrusts, she lifted up her bottle of beer to take a swig.

In 1996, a Florida man filed a lawsuit against a strip joint where he claimed to have received neck injuries at the "hands" of one Tawny Peaks and her size 69HH breasts.

Unfortunately, this time it was obvious that he had become a little, um, excited. His package made contact with her bottle, and her bottle, in turn, made contact with her tooth enamel. Guess what won?

Allie jumped up screaming, "Oh my God, my toof! My toof!"

She rushed over to the mirror shouting, "He chipped my toof! My teef are ruined!" She immediately grabbed a nail file and started going to town filing her new snaggle tooth. The stripper was really embarrassed. Besides chipping the birthday girl's tooth, I think he realized just how into the strip we knew he

According to Dr. Kendra Novick, DDS, this type of dental trauma is common and can be treated easily with composite bonding for roughly two hundred dollars.

was getting, due to the excitement that was showing through his man thong.

Needless to say, the strip was over. The next challenge was coming up with a good story for Allie to tell her parents and her dentist to explain how she'd chipped off a good portion of her front tooth.

—*Western Washington University*

LESSON LEARNED: You get what you pay for. That old cliché is true when it comes to both seafood and strippers. A little bank would make the difference between a Chippendale and a chipped tooth.

Hooters and Honors

I was working at Hooters when this man came in to celebrate his fifty-second birthday. Our job as Hooters girls is to make sure that the customer has fun, so all the other girls and I decided to take *customer service* to the next level that night. We announced to everyone that we had a birthday boy in the house, then we turned up the music, jumped up on the bar, and started to dance for him. I chose to take it a step further, though, and I reached behind the counter, grabbed the water gun, and started to spray the girls' little white T-shirts. Then I gave "Birthday Boy" the pleasure of spraying mine. It was sexy and fun, and the crowd went crazy!

> According to Hooters' website, "The women's rights movement is important because it guarantees women have the right to choose their own careers, be it a Supreme Court Justice or Hooters Girl."

Birthday Boy was speechless. All he could do was blush in response to our show. But he did give me a huge tip. As he was leaving, Birthday Boy kissed me on the cheek and called me "brilliant."

Well, it was the first day of fall semester. Everything was cool until I walked into my English class and saw Birthday Boy at the front introducing himself as Professor T. Franke. I couldn't believe it! The next day I walked up to his desk to turn in my first homework assignment. When he took my paper, he looked at it briefly, then looked at me and said, "I'm glad I now know your name. I didn't want to spend the semester calling you Hooters Girl!" I was so embarrassed!

—*Montgomery College*

LESSON LEARNED: As the last two stories so effectively demonstrate, using sex appeal and your dance of a thousand ta-tas to make a quick buck can lead to embarrassment in myriad ways.

Caught Hot-Handed

A friend and I were having dinner one night at one of the local bar/restaurants. I went to use the restroom and began washing my hands. I turned on the hot water and nearly scalded my hands. I could barely touch the water, it was so hot. I turned the hot water off and washed with cold water.

A safe temperature for tap water is 110 degrees Fahrenheit. Exposure to water at this temperature will result in third-degree burns in approximately ten hours. Even though this is a "relatively safe" temperature, the human pain threshold is around 106–108 degrees Fahrenheit.

I went back to the table and told my story to my friend Allan. He repeatedly called me a "wussy," until I'd simply had enough and threw down the gauntlet: "If you can hold your hands underneath this hot water for ten seconds, I'll give you a hundred dollars."

"What if you win?" he asked.

"You buy my drinks for the rest of the night," I replied.

He jumped up from the table, and we both went to the bathroom like a couple of sorority girls on a double date. He turned on the hot water tap. "Ready, set, go!"

I watched as he plunged his hands under the water, looked back at my watch to check the time, and then looked back at his hands. He had jerked them back from the water in less than three seconds. Now, he was the one complaining like the big wussy!

After discussing how dangerous this was over the newly purchased round of drinks, we plotted how we could turn this newfound faucet of fire into a windfall of cash! We scripted the "good cop/bad cop" routine we would use the next time we found ourselves together in that men's room.

The following Friday, we were partying at the same bar. During our first trip to the bathroom, I bet my friend a hundred dollars that he couldn't hold his hands under the water for thirty seconds. After he backed down, I (loudly) offered the same bet to anyone within earshot.

Unlucky soul number one bellied up to the sink, and sure enough he didn't last more than five seconds. I suddenly felt a certain amount of guilt setting in. It was one thing to burn my friend after he'd called me a wussy, but another to knowingly entrap a stranger into our devilish plot. I let the red-handed fool off by having him buy me a beer.

When I got back to the table, my friend admonished me for not making the guy pay. "He knew what he was getting into. He would've made you pay. Dude, you've gotta do it again, and make them pay!" I reluctantly agreed, and later that night we found ourselves back at the scene of the crime. After throwing the bait out there again, we had our second daring young fool ready to show us how tough he was.

I looked down to make sure his hands were—get this—cupped. Steam rose from the sink so thickly that it steamed up the mirror. I looked down at my watch. This guy had passed the previously set record of three seconds easily—we were now at five seconds, and then at ten. I looked down at his hands to make sure he wasn't "cheating" by allowing the water to flow through his fingers or something. Unfortunately, he wasn't.

I looked at his face to get some sort of reaction. Hell, the first guy had let out a yell like a schoolgirl when we turned on the water. Our new hero was stone-faced. He wasn't making a noise, nor was he moving at all. I looked down at my watch, and—I'll be damned. He was going to make it. The second hand on my watch read twenty-five seconds. Shit! We had met our match!

I looked over to my friend with a look of disbelief. He turned and left the restroom. I began counting down, "Okay, dude, you're halfway there." I wasn't going to give in that easy—hell, these were the longest seconds of his life, and he'd never know the difference anyway. I figured that if I told him he had endured all of that pain but still had just as long to go for the gold, he would fold like a deck of cards.

I looked again for a reaction, and this guy wasn't with us. He was staring deep into the mirror, not moving, not making a sound. "Twenty-seven, twenty-eight, twenty-nine, thirty!" A loud yell of congratulations and clapping erupted from the small crowd now gathered around the sink cheering on our new hero. He had actually lasted more than forty seconds. This was no man, this was a legend.

I broke the news to him that I didn't have the money on me, and that I'd have to go to the ATM. I asked him to accompany me so he'd know I wasn't trying to skip out on him.

As we got out of the bar, he explained that he was able to ignore the pain thanks to his experience as a rock climber. I nodded and congratulated him again as I pulled his hundred dollars out of the ATM. As I gave it to him, I noticed that his hands were as red as tomatoes. Blisters had developed and were heavily oozing a clear substance.

As we walked back into the bar, I offered to buy him a beer. He agreed. As I handed him a Heineken, I noticed that he was shaking like a leaf. He cuddled the beer as if it were a teddy bear, and thanked me. I congratulated him one more time and went out to the patio, where my friends were. I told them the story, and they all laughed at me.

About this time, we heard sirens. Cops, fire trucks, and an ambulance came flying to the front of the bar. With all three factions of civil service rushing in, we assumed there had been a fight. Not more than a few minutes later, the paramedics wheeled out a gurney with our hero lying on it with both hands sticking straight out. The paramedics had bandaged up his hands so much that they looked like two gigantic Q-tips.

As they wheeled him into the ambulance and drove him off, I wondered if this was how he saw his evening shaping up when he went out that night. I found solace in the fact that he had a hundred dollars in cash to put toward the hospital bill, although I wasn't sure how he was going to get it out of his pocket.

> "I learned that no matter how funny a prank may be, a certain amount of guilt is inevitable when someone gets hurt—even if it was his own damn fault that he took the bet," adds author Brad Fritz.

—*University of Oklahoma*

LESSON LEARNED: You can turn anything into a moneymaking scam. These guys showed great industry and ingenuity. Of course, they didn't expect to face the Kryptonite to industry and ingenuity: pure insanity.

CHAPTER 12

Lady Luck's Biatch

Criticism of Bad Bets, Stupid Dares

The great American philosopher Kenny Rogers taught the world two things. First, you got to know when to hold 'em, know when to fold 'em. Second, a man with a creepy beard can still make tasty chicken. Unfortunately, for many a college student, that first lesson still needs to sink in. Bad bets and dumb dares are a common theme in a lot of our stories.

Smart risk assessment is not a universally understood concept. What else would explain the degree of danger and embarrassment to which students will subject themselves in the name of a bet . . . and for mere pocket change? One can only hope these students will one day learn either that "winning" is not worth risking bodily injury, or that they should hold out for a lot more dough.

Check out the following stories to see how our beloved students fare against both Lady Luck and a flaming urethra. But, please, no wagering.

The Pepper and the Pecker

There are many things that are typically associated with a good college story: alcohol, sex, drugs, etc. What makes this story interesting is the introduction of a unique variable. A very spicy variable. A habañero pepper.

After a basketball game one night, several friends and I met up at a house where I was doing some house-sitting. There were four of us, most notably a strapping young lad named Lance Roberts. The four of us got to drinking, as college students will do. After we had each consumed

> The habañero chili is over one hundred times hotter than a jalapeño pepper, which, by the way, should also not be shoved in your pee hole.

a few tasty beverages, I noticed a pepper sitting on the counter by the refrigerator. It was a habañero pepper—one of the hottest peppers in the world, capable of making whoever ingests it experience the mother of all lava shits.

Well, being semi-inebriated, I thought it would be fun if we each chewed up a seed from the pepper. We did. It was painful, but one seed wasn't enough to do any serious damage. I wasn't satisfied. "Hey Lance!" I yelled (unnecessarily, since he was standing next to me). "Why don't you shove the rest of that pepper up your ass?"

Lance replied, as expected, with a resounding, "Fuck no! That shit burns your ass bad enough after you *eat* it." As an afterthought, he added, "And I don't like the idea of putting a pepper that size in my butt. A pepper of *any* size . . ."

> Mule: An individual, often male, who doesn't give a shit about his dignity or safety and will accept any bet or challenge against his better judgment.

I could see his point; we weren't nearly drunk enough to start putting foreign objects in our asses. However, I had twenty dollars in my pocket, a tempting sum of money for a poor college student. "Okay, Lance, no pepper in the bad place," I said. "But how about just one seed?"

"One seed, in my ass?" Lance asked, contemplating this.

"No. In your dick," I replied. I was feeling twisted.

Again I received a powerful response: "Fuck you! Nothing's going in my dick, especially not that spicy piece of Satan!"

"I'll give you twenty dollars."

"Okay."

Lance dropped his pants and grabbed a seed. "Are you guys really gonna watch me stuff this in my dick?" he asked us.

"Are you kidding?" I replied. "Apart from this being the coolest thing I've ever witnessed, I've got twenty dollars on this. There's no way I'm going to let you 'pretend' to 'spice-ify' your pee hole. I'm making sure you shove that seed in there good and deep."

Seeing that he was out of time for stalling, Lance pulled out his dick and shoved in the pepper seed. He stood for a moment, with the seed still nestled inside his penis, and said calmly, "Man, that was the easiest twenty dollars I ever ma . . ."

I assume that the word that he left unfinished was supposed to be "made," but he never got that far. His jaw dropped, and his eyes bulged. His face expressed a feeling of horror and torment that I'm sure most men will never know.

He began to scream and ran from the room. I quickly followed him. He ran into a side bedroom and jumped completely over the bed. It's important to note that all of this was done with his pants around his ankles, and was therefore an amazing display of athleticism.

While still in the air from his leap, Luke grabbed a bottle of lotion off the nightstand and, still before hitting the ground, began to squirt the lotion all over his crotch. When he landed, he rubbed his genitals with a ferocity that can only be brought on by a severely burned urethra.

Rather than stay on the floor with the comfort of the lotion, Lance ran back to the living room, where he continued to scream and rub himself. Only now, he was screaming in pain on the futon, rolling back and forth and now wearing only his shirt. Fifteen minutes later, he was still screaming. It was the best twenty dollars I'd ever spent.

As a side note, I neglected to tell the homeowners about the naked, lotion-covered man in severe pain who had soiled their futon.

—*Pacific Lutheran University*

LESSON LEARNED: Take a bet only if the payout is worth the exposure. It's Gambling 101 here, folks. And no matter how you look at it, damaging your precious pee hole isn't worth anywhere near twenty dollars. Twenty-one dollars, on the other hand, could be a totally different story.

The Power Twister

This is a tale of the bad things that can happen when the laws of physics get the best of you, a tale of how the geeky guy down the hall can wind up with a large hole in his face. But I'm getting ahead of myself. Let's start from the beginning, shall we?

I lived up on the hill on the Assumption campus, in a place called A Dorm. The dorm has another name now, but back then it was one of three mini-dorms that were also coed. I lived on the second floor with my room-mate, Jason, a guy we nicknamed Lippy the Leopard, for no particular reason. Jason was in USMC ROTC and was pretty hard-core, but a nice guy all around.

"Semper Fi" translated from Latin means "Always Faithful."

I give Jason full credit for introducing us to the Power Twister. The Power Twister was an ingenious device. It consisted of two metal pipes joined in the middle by a heavy metal spring. To build muscle, you simply bent the pipes together.

The simple device became a permanent fixture in our dorm room. The damn thing worked, too. Cranking the spring over and over was a pretty good upper-body workout. But it was during dorm room drinking games that the Power Twister really shone.

Fast forward a few weeks. Jason, a few other guys, and I were having a couple of beers, watching the Bruins, and passing the device around, challenging one another to top the latest record for consecutive spring-flexes.

That was when Disco Dave walked into the room. Dave weighed all of a hundred pounds. He was the proud owner of a collection of neon poly-ester shirts and the meanest tight-curl perm this side of Greg Brady! When he saw the Power Twister, a maniacal look came over him and he steadfastly challenged Jason to a duel.

Jason cranked the device ten times in rapid succession. Dave, surprisingly, did the same.

Jason arched an intrigued eyebrow in a way that suggested Joe Don Baker crossed with Mr. Spock. He'd underestimated the Disco King. He put the Power Twister behind his back and cranked it. Dave took it and did the same.

We were impressed. But Jason wasn't about to be beaten. You know,

Semper Fi and all that. He took the contraption from Dave, bent it until the two bars touched, and then transferred it to one hand and held it out before him, almost as a bizarre and terrible object of worship.

The room grew silent. We looked on in awe.

Jason carefully transferred the Power Twister back to both hands and released the tension, moving the handles back to their 180-degree position.

Dave grinned and took the exerciser. He grimaced and grunted, and put all his muscle into it. He bent the bars until they touched, then transferred all that potential energy to one hand, held the Power Twister out before him, and broke into a broad smile.

And that's when he lost his grip.

The Power Twister uncoiled with a sound like a gunshot, the metal bar springing through the air with an audible whiplash . . . and catching him full in the mouth. Blood and teeth flew through the air. Dave went down as if he'd been shot.

Everyone gathered around him. After a second, Dave stood up, both hands over his mouth. Jason asked if he was okay, and he nodded, "Yes." But when he pulled his hands away, part of his face was missing.

There was a hole about the size of a quarter on his lower right cheek. He didn't even know it was there until he saw our faces all turn gray. Then, slowly, inquisitively, he poked his tongue around inside his mouth.

And his tongue poked right through the hole.

Man, was that gross!

We took him over to City Hospital and got him stitched up. After that, the Power Twister was retired—for the good of all humanity.

—*Assumption College*

LESSON LEARNED: Just about anything, if handled with reckless stupidity, can do bodily damage. This is a universal theme, as we've seen: pepper seed and an exercise device have each kicked some ass. Let's just pray these guys stay away from explosives.

Pizzalicious

College is a time when many students test the limits of their bodies, whether through lack of sleep, heavy drinking, or an all–ramen noodle diet. Senior year, my buddy A.J. and I found a new way to abuse our-selves. A local pizzeria was holding a contest: If two people could eat an absurdly enormous twenty-nine-inch pizza in under an hour, they'd get the pizza for free. The restaurant didn't offer a cash prize, a gift certifi-cate, or even a T-shirt, just a free pizza. Of course, this was all the in-centive we needed, and we decided to take our best shot at immortality.

> On July 11, 2005, Rich LeFevre won the Bacci Pizza Eating Contest by downing seven Bacci jumbo slices of pizza in fifteen minutes.

A.J. and I did everything in our power to increase our chances of finish-ing the pizza, which we calculated was the equivalent of approximately three seventeen-inch pizzas. We began a strict eating and exercise regi-men, and consulted our friend and future doctor Patrick on whether eat-ing the cheese or the crust first would improve our chances.

When the hour arrived, we rounded up about ten friends who were in-terested in cheering us on (and witnessing our foolishness in action). In the cheering section was A.J.'s girlfriend, Allison, who was blissfully un-aware of the extent of the gluttony that would soon take place.

The pizza arrived at our table amid much hoopla, and I was immedi-ately alarmed by the significantly thicker-than-anticipated crust on our gi-gantic pizza, which took up the entire table. Nonetheless, we were determined in our quest and launched out to a fast start, completing half the pizza in a mere twenty minutes. Our prospects looked bright.

As we attacked the second half of the pizza, however, we began to "hit the wall." Worse yet, after a few more minutes of gorging ourselves, the wall fell on top of us with a resounding thud. Desperate to catch a second

> Food condition: The dramatic ups and downs that come from not eating all day, then gorging oneself. Symptoms range from crankiness to hyperactivity to pure insanity.

wind, A.J. stumbled to the bathroom to induce some vomiting, only to find that management had locked the men's bathroom as a precaution-ary measure. Unfazed, he entered the women's bathroom and un-leashed a massive regurgitation. Face flushed and eyes watery, he emerged from the bathroom ready to reattack as several petrified patrons looked on.

Following A.J.'s lead, I entered the bathroom but found my efforts to pull the trigger fruitless. When I exited, I tried to fire myself up with a bizarre combination of jumping up and down, pounding my chest, and storming about the room. The restaurant employees took the opportunity to needle us by recalling that two 120-pound women had polished off the pizza earlier that week. Sinking to our lowest level, we then took the unlikely advice of a friend who told us that eating mint Tic Tacs was a surefire way to increase our appetites.

With ten minutes to go, I was about halfway through my last (14.5-inch) slice, but with a mountain of crust left on my plate. I raised my weary head about an inch and saw that A.J. was also about halfway through his slice. Unfortunately, he had another full slice to go. He looked at me with glazed eyes and said, "You're going to have to finish that last slice." I knew then that we were doomed, but we gallantly pushed forward to the end. Despite our best efforts, the twenty-nine-inch pizza had ultimately turned out to be more than even A.J. and I could handle.

We were so stuffed we could barely move, and after forking over twenty-five dollars for the pizza, we staggered out to the mall parking lot as our friends looked on and laughed. As A.J. stood hunched over a random car and attempted to stave off vomiting, I used my remaining strength to toss my car keys to Allison and informed her that I was no longer able to operate heavy machinery. Being the trouper she was, Allison took pity on me and agreed to drive us home.

During the fifteen-minute ride, A.J. lay in the backseat moaning in pain as Allison stared ahead with a grim visage. I sat in the front seat with my head dangling out the window and the wind rushing through my hair, praying for a digestive miracle that would end my suffering.

When we arrived home, A.J. hopped out and began spitting on the concrete. Allison, who had been extraordinarily patient throughout our foolishness, was reaching the end of her leash. "I hardly think this is an appropriate place to throw up," she said, presumably suggesting that A.J. take his vomiting into the privacy of his apartment. Instead, he walked around the side of a nearby apartment building and resumed his upchucking. Allison had seen enough and beat a hasty exit as I looked on and laughed . . . but not for long. Within a few minutes I, too, was unleashing the most powerful vomit of my young life, as my stomach rebelled against the excesses I had delivered upon it.

Our final combined tally: seven slices of pizza (traditional pizza equivalent: twenty-one slices), nine bouts of vomiting, two mint Tic Tacs ingested, and one frantic trip to the ladies' bathroom.

It was a full six months before I could even look at a slice of pizza without feeling queasy.

—*Wake Forest University*

Alumni Update: The author made a full recovery from this experience, even going on an all-pizza diet during a subsequent trip to Italy. In between the occasional bouts of power eating, he found time to co-write this book. As for A.J. and Allison, they overcame this unfortunate episode and are now happily married.

LESSON LEARNED: Not all mountains are meant to be climbed. With the energy and wild abandon of youth, everything is a stunt waiting to happen. Later in life, you realize that you'll never play pro ball, that the cross-country trip in a go-cart won't take place, and that competitive eating is best left to small Japanese kids.

CHAPTER 13

One Giant Step Back

A Survey of Just Dumb Moves

Stupidity is a many-splendored thing and a muse for many great college stories. How do people so heavily tested slip through the cracks and act so unreasonably?

It's surprising how many students are a few credits short of a full course load, so to speak. We can only hope that they mature and wise up later in life—and never, ever get accepted into medical school. Some of these students shouldn't be around the rubber gloves, let alone the scalpels.

But that's the beauty of college. If you can keep your book smarts at the acceptable minimum, you can pretty much ignore everything else and still make it through. So sorry, Darwin, we've found a loophole. Just keep the species on an enclosed property with a regular supply of food, and fitness is no longer part of the survival equation.

Maybe the most important lesson is that it's okay to be dumb. Go ahead, embrace your idiocy: forget about a rotting pumpkin, be careless during science lab, do the stuff dumb people do. Embarrassment is only temporary.

So now we have the chance to examine this idiotic behavior up close and personal. Enjoy these tidbits of foolishness and see if maybe Darwin was right after all.

Weird Science

This story took place during my second year at university. I was studying chemistry, a class that went toward my BS degree. As chemistry is a very hands-on subject, the practical labs made up a crucial part of the course. A good friend of mine, Rod, and I were put together in a lab group for one of our Inorganic Chemistry papers. Rod, in his own words, is a "top man," always ready for fun (infamous for his naked runs around his hall of residence, etc.). However, he's also quite a brain and does very well in chemistry—at least in the theory!

This one particular lab, we were dealing with a compound called titanium tetrachloride ($TiCl_4$). It reacts violently with water and is corrosive as hell; in general, it's bloody nasty stuff. They issue it to you in little sealed glass ampoules. You have to snap off the top while wearing safety glasses, a lab coat, rubber gloves, and a full-face mask. In addition to this, you have to do the whole thing in a fume cupboard, with the safety shield pulled down as far as possible. You get the idea.

$TiCl_4$ has been used to create naval smokescreens. If we told you any more, we'd have to kill you.

Rod (being on the ball) was getting right into his preparation. He was one of the first in the class to get up to the stage where the $TiCl_4$ was added. He put on all the safety gear, with the exception of the lab coat (uh-oh), and took his ampoule from the technician. Quite a few of us in the class gathered around to watch, so Rod had quite an audience. He nervously took the ampoule in his hand and proceeded to snap off the top. That's when all hell broke loose.

The next thing I knew, I was watching Rod run like hell toward the sink, screaming for help from the lab supervisor. "Dr. Beemur, Dr. Beemur! I just got this all over my hands, AND ALL OVER MY CROTCH!"

Rod was at the sink, furiously trying to wash the stuff off his hands and spraying water all over his jeans (which is a dumb idea because $TiCl_4$ reacts with water). Smoke and gas began taking over the room. It turned out that the entire ampoule had shattered in Rod's hand, instead of breaking off cleanly at the top.

Dr. Beemur grabbed Rod by his arm and dragged him—wailing his head off, mind you—into the back room. Meanwhile, all of us in the classroom were laughing our asses off. Five minutes later, Rod reappeared, this time wearing a lab coat with a mere two inches of boxer shorts hanging out underneath. His jeans were draped over his arm. The $TiCl_4$ had burned right through them!

What we didn't know at the time was that, while in the back room, Dr. Beemur had had to give Rod a "burns inspection," aka checking that Rod hadn't burnt his schlong. How did it feel, I wondered, having your tackle *inspected* by a lecturer?

Anyway, by that time the whole class had gathered around to find out what was going on. When we saw Rod in his boxers, we just lost it. The whole class just fell about laughing. Poor Rod was so embarrassed that he ran off to his hostel to have a shower and change his clothes. Unfortunately for him, the hostel was a good three hundred meters away, and it was a windy day. The wind blew his lab coat up, exposing his undergarments as he sprinted up Symonds Street, one of the busiest roads in Auckland.

On top of everything else, in his panic Rod had forgotten to take off his safety glasses. So there was this guy running up the road in broad daylight, looking like some kind of chemist turned streaker. He must have been quite a sight—he's lucky he didn't get himself arrested as well!

—*Auckland University of Technology*

Alumni Update: "Rod's okay; he's still a hard-core chemist. He's now studying toward his doctorate in chemistry, as a matter of fact. According to him, the family jewels are still in good nick (but we'll have to see kids to believe this). Even as Dr. Rod, I think he'll stay as far away from the $TiCl_4$ as he can!"

LESSON LEARNED: Haste makes for dissolving genitals. This may also be a case of karma punishing someone who showed off in chemistry class. So don't showboat in lab, for Pete's sake—actually, maybe it should be for Rod's sack.

The Pumpkin Bomb

We were sitting around drinking one day (because it was Tuesday), and my roommate took it upon himself to secure a pumpkin to carve for

Halloween. We informed him of the ludicrousness of this suggestion, as it was only late September. Unfazed, he came back from the dining hall bearing a fine-ass thirty-pound pumpkin, and we all agreed that his pumpkin-carving idea was a good one.

In the course of the next month, the pumpkin was moved about the suite, ultimately ending up in a university-provided chair. Since we had no use for said chair at the time—for we had far superior La-Z-Boys—the pumpkin remained there until the morning before Halloween (more than a month later). The day before Halloween, we were drinking again (because it was Thursday). It was just one of those days when you start drinking the instant you leave class, perhaps cracking open a beer on the way home, then stopping at a friend's to enjoy a few more.

> Carved pumpkins last longer when you apply a light coating of petroleum jelly to the cuts.

I got home and decided to take a shower. It just so happened that my roommate was walking back from the bathroom right at that moment. We passed each other and simultaneously stopped, sniffed, and said, "What the *fuck* is that smell?" It was bad—like something had died overnight in the heater.

Up until that point in the semester, neither he nor I had paid much attention to the upkeep of our room—much to the frustration of the cleaning staff. Now we were both rummaging around on our hands and knees, trying to find the source of the stench. Five minutes passed, and all we had found with smell-generating potential was a half-full, dust-blanketed 40 behind the couch and a mummified pizza. I took responsibility, leaned in, and sniffed . . . no smell.

In our zeal, we had forgotten the pumpkin, which was still sitting comfortably in the chair.

We both looked at it suspiciously. Then at each other. With a shrug, my roommate lifted the pumpkin . . . and with an unmistakable *shloop*, the shell of the pumpkin lifted away, leaving the pumpkin's rotting guts in the chair. At the same moment, a cloud of evil little fruit flies was set free.

> The average American college student produces 640 pounds of garbage a year—not including freakishly huge rotting pumpkins.

After more than a month of feasting on our prize vegetable, they were pretty frisky. My roommate, holding a rapidly disintegrating pumpkin shell in his hands, gagged loudly. I coughed and, to the best of my ability, tried to shoo the flies out the open window.

> The life cycle of a fruit fly from egg to adult is approximately ten days.

At this point in the story, I feel I should mention that my roommate was prone to sudden, direct, and unconscious action when faced with a problem . . .

He heaved the rotting vegetable out of our fifth-floor window.

The pumpkin hit bottom with a *splud,* followed by the tinkling of broken glass. Fearing the worst, I warily looked out the window and immediately collapsed in laughter.

Obviously, there was justice in this world. The pumpkin bomb had struck dead center on a new "I'm Daddy's girl" black Volvo station wagon, blowing out two of the windows upon impact. As drunk as we were, we thought it was the funniest thing on the planet. My roommate, exhibiting his talent for shifting blame and generally getting away with it, closed our window, ran upstairs to the suite directly above ours and, upon finding it unlocked, opened their window. By the way, he remained wearing nothing but his towel the entire time.

The authorities investigating the case had a hard time believing that the docile freshmen girls who shared that suite had an affection for hurling pumpkins out of windows, and thus the incident has gone officially unsolved to this day.

—*Case Western Reserve University*

LESSON LEARNED: Again we see that anything can be used to create havoc—and nasty stank. Whether with cunning resourcefulness (see the last chapter) or apathetic neglect (as in this story), it's amazing how college students can turn almost anything into a weapon of mass messiness.

Rug and the Monkey Sheep

Upon arriving in central New Hampshire for my first semester at Plymouth State University, I learned I had been randomly assigned to live with a guy from Haverhill, Massachusetts, named Rug Hammly.

"My teammates call me 'The Vacuum,' " Rug announced as we unpacked our stuff in the dorm room. "Because I really know how to clean up on the field." Silly me for thinking "Rug" was his nickname.

Rug was a three-hundred-pound, bald-headed offensive lineman on the football team who would proudly declare to anyone who'd listen that his major at school was "kickin' ass," with a minor in "takin' names."

> Hall of Fame third baseman Brooks Robinson was nicknamed "the Human Vacuum Cleaner" because of his outstanding defense.

One night, during a community builder at our dorm, Rug asked me to be his partner for an activity. I accepted because I really didn't want to insult anyone of his immense size and stature. Figuring that the safest game being played that evening was "Guess the Rebus," I suggested we give it a shot. I explained to Rug that a rebus was a puzzle that used pictures of objects to represent words or phrases. This prompted a look of confusion from him, but it was quickly replaced by a hefty, gluttonous smile.

"Wouldn't it be sweet if titties was one of the pictures?" he hooted, slapping me hard on the shoulder.

When it was our turn to play, I was the one selected to arrange the rebus on the board, while Rug had forty-five seconds to write down his guess on a piece of paper. I was given my own scrap of paper with the word "scapegoat" written on it. Reaching into the bag of images supplied for the game, I pulled out a picture of an ape and a goat and positioned them in that order on the board.

Even Rug would figure this puzzle out, I assumed. The names of the animals were printed on the bottom of the cards, for God sake.

> Some of the earliest examples of rebuses have been found in letters written in the sixth century B.C. in Ephesus, a city of ancient Greece.

Rug leaned forward in his chair and squinted up at the board with the focus and intensity of a mathematics professor during the screening of a doctoral thesis. When he flung himself up out of his seat and, yelling and pointing in my direction, demanded to know what the hell a "monkey sheep" was, I decided I should start thinking of a polite way to weasel out of playing Pictionary with him.

It was going to be a long year.

—*Plymouth State University*

LESSON LEARNED: Here's the ugly truth about living with humans who aren't you: Other people's stupidity will be a constant theme throughout your life. And the more thickheaded they are, the more likely they'll be your work supervisor or next-door neighbor—only without a cool name like Rug.

THE PARTY

No party is any fun unless seasoned with folly.
—Desiderius Erasmus, Dutch Renaissance scholar

The college party is an ancient art. It has been an institution as long as there have been students and dorms—and kegs to be sneaked by the former into the latter. From frat houses to abandoned warehouses, from student athletes to student mathletes, the party threads through every aspect of college life.

One can dismiss college parties simply as an excuse for young people to overindulge in illicit substances, gyrate their sweaty loins to mindless music, and damage public property. And of course, this would be correct. But the party also represents a training ground for social life. It's about learning how to negotiate (for beer), how to lead people (to line up for beer), and how to inspire greatness (to hide the beer before the cops come). The party represents the critical transitional stage between the playground and the meet-and-greet with the big client.

In the following chapters, we delve into the social hierarchy and subversive ingenuity of the college party. But don't worry, it's not going to be that boring.

CHAPTER 14

Thinking Outside the Box of Wine

Advanced Party Techniques

Of course there are parties without alcohol, and there are many dry dorms where students play board games and debate erudite topics. If you're reading this book, that's most likely not your scene. Sure, those stiffs will rule the world and lap us in the salary race, but we'll know how to wave our hands in the air like we just don't care.

This pursuit of fun can teach a lesson or two in creative thinking—and creative rule breaking. The party is a canvas upon which the exceptional students display their artistry and test their limits. As with the grain punch being served, parties involve taking everyday ingredients and re-configuring them into fresh—albeit chemically inconvenienced—experiences. So why waste all of that good thinking and creativity on filling blue books when you have an indoor beach party to throw?

Consider yourself invited to this celebration of inspired celebrations. (But please, don't invite too many dudes.) And remember: It's not just about getting this party started. It's about getting this party started *right*.

Indoor Winter Beach Party

For spring break, I took a trip back home to Puerto Rico with my five room-mates from Penn State. A week of sun, women, and alcohol. Yet, surprisingly, the real story began the weekend after our return. Friday night the temperature was below zero, and there was no way we were gonna go out in that weather and ruin our post–spring break spirit.

One of my crazy roommates got the most fascinating idea: Let's have a beach party . . . in our apartment! Wow. That was the best idea this guy had come up with all semester.

The largest indoor beach is in the Ocean Dome in Miyazaki, Japan. Its fake ocean holds 13,500 tons of water.

We all jumped in my Maxima and drove to Lowe's to purchase a whopping eight hundred pounds of sand. Then it was on to KB Toys, where we bought two ten-person-capacity pools and lifeguard shirts—for safety reasons, naturally.

Back at our apartment, we poured the sand all over the rug and filled the pools with hot water. Some people walking by our place became so excited about the prospect of a beach party in the dead of winter that a few even helped us with the preparations.

At 10:00 P.M., everyone started showing up in their bathing suits—hot girls all over the place, loud music, liquor everywhere, water splashing. It was the mother of all parties. At about 1:00 A.M., however, there came a banging on our door. I opened the door a crack and was greeted by our downstairs neighbor. He immediately began screaming at me. "What the fuck? It's pouring in my apartment!" Then I opened my door a little more, and he saw what was going on inside.

"Screw my apartment!" he said, promptly stripping off his jeans and jumping in the pool.

About thirty minutes later, the cops showed up, as usual, to bust our party and deliver a summons. When Officer Slater walked into the apartment, I thought, "Shit, I'm going to jail for this!" The music stopped, and the whole crowd went dead silent. Visions of an evening in the slammer flashed before me.

But then I took a closer look at the officer's face, and he appeared to be wearing an expression of amusement. I couldn't believe it. The officer actually congratulated me! He shook my hand and told me that this was the best damn party he had ever seen. He actually asked if he could join us later when his shift was over, but he never did.

I couldn't believe it. I had beaten the system and thought we were safe. Nope. Again, there was banging on our door, this time accompanied by screaming. When I opened the door, I found myself face-to-face with a girl soaked in water. She was another neighbor from downstairs. Without hesitating, she grabbed me in a forceful manner and took me down to her place.

Holy shit! There was a waterfall on her wall, her rug was floating, and pans had been placed around the room to catch the innumerable leaks. I could muster no words of condolence except to invite her up to my party. Alas, this failed to placate her, and she started flipping out. She threatened to sue me, have me evicted, and all sorts of other unpleasantries. I decided she would be best dealt with in the morning and I beat a hasty retreat back to the party.

Around 4:00 A.M., people started to leave, and we turned on the lights. Wow. We had never stopped to think that sand and water created mud. And it was everywhere, in the kitchen, in the hallway, on the beds, on the pillows—EVERYWHERE.

We had never thought about the cleaning process either. As drunk as we all were, we headed to Giant Food and rented an industrial vacuum.

We arrived back home to find one of my roommates fighting and struggling with one of the pools. It was leaking big time, with all the water going downstairs. But, what the hell, my downstairs neighbor (the happy guy, not the water-soaked girl) was totally passed out on the couch. It took us twenty-four hours straight of cleaning to get the place back in order.

Miraculously, we got that apartment spic and span. The following Monday we were all watching TV when all of a sudden we heard someone banging on the door. It was the landlord. He'd heard about our party, and he was furious. He walked in, looked at the apartment, and walked into the rooms, but he seemed confused. Then he confronted us. We denied everything. Meanwhile, the hallway rug had footstep marks going into our apartment. I have no idea how he hadn't noticed this.

Then he started bitching about how all the pipes in the building were clogged from so much sand. Poor guy. We had destroyed his building, which was one of the most popular ones at Penn State.

Not surprisingly, we became the most popular crowd at school. To this day, four years later, when I visit PSU I actually meet people who know of me because of that party. Some people are even honored to meet me, usually the freshmen.

> Drano's Max Gel Clog Remover claims to be "Safe for all pipes, it's also the best at removing hair, soap scum, and other gunky clogs." No mention of sand.

In retrospect, it's unbelievable that we escaped arrest and eviction. But I'll tell you what, it feels nice to be recognized and to remember those great memories!

—Pennsylvania State University

LESSON LEARNED: As a visionary, prepare to be misunderstood. Edison, Einstein, Popeil—all were geniuses whose ideas—and rotisseries—faced the criticism of naysayers and skeptics. But did that stop them? No! So don't let landlords or neighbors or the law stop you.

Party Goes Up, Party Goes Down

Messiah was a goody-two-shoes Christian college where smoking and drinking were not allowed and opposite-sex dorm visits were limited to fifteen hours per week, so we had to get creative.

One night, at around 3:00 A.M., a couple of us were awake with nothing to do. So we went to the North Complex: three dorms joined by a main lobby. Mischievous ideas came to us as we observed the huge cargo elevator with doors on both sides.

> German inventor Werner von Siemens built the first electric elevator in 1880.

We took half the furniture from a lobby—a couch, a coffee table, chairs, and a small potted tree—and put it in the elevator, setting it up like a little living room. We also brought in a big cooler, some cards, and magazines. We kept the booze hidden in the couch because we were all underage. It was really quite something, if I do say so myself.

We chilled in our new living room for several hours. The best part was when the whole room would start to rise or fall suddenly, then stop. The doors would open, and there would be some half-awake person in front of the elevator. Invariably, this poor soul would stand there wide-eyed, wondering if his eyes were playing tricks on him. A few people actually stood there without saying anything until the door closed again, and the whole time, we acted as if nothing unusual were going on. It's amazing we didn't bust out laughing every time the door opened.

—*Messiah College*

LESSON LEARNED: Dream big. Dream bold. If you dream of hosting an elevator party, do it. If you want to bring peace to the Middle East or save the rain forest, that little stuff is good, too.

Magic Carpet Ride

Emerson College has a motto: "Expression necessary to evolution," and the student body truly lives by these words . . . kinda. The school is a melting pot for the creative, bizarre, and magical. I use the word "magical" because my best friend in college was an actual magician. I immediately befriended him after we both performed in an orientation show for incoming freshmen. I was a sophomore doing stand-up, and he was a junior making bunnies disappear.

Matt is from the South, and I assumed that, like his act, he was a clean-cut American magician. He was full of puns, which he uttered in his deep Southern accent, and actually quite good at what he did. In fact, he had become one of the top children's entertainers in the country, making six figures a year. He had more money than he knew what to do with, which is always a bad thing for a twenty-year-old kid in one of the coolest cities in America. I would come to find that, most of the time, he blew all of it on drugs, strippers, foam bunnies, limos, and strippers. But before I knew this, we were just performing buddies.

Shortly after we met, Matt introduced me to his friend/mentor Ned Garcia, who was several years older than Matt and also a children's magician.

It wasn't long after I met Ned that I realized that he and Matt were not just magicians. Ned was somewhat of a pimp, and Matt was his sidekick. During my first trip to his apartment,

> The magician's oath includes a promise never to perform any illusion without first practicing the effect.

Ned lit up one of the fattest joints I had ever seen as he divulged his plans for an upcoming party. Matt also started smoking pot. I didn't know Matt that well, but it was Tuesday, and he was from Mayberry! Pot smoking was not something white-bread magicians with red freckles should be doing before hump day.

Me: "Do you do anything else?"

Matt: "Sure. I did coke, but I was on acid, and it was during a magic convention in Vegas, so it didn't take. . . . Wanna hit?"

I was stunned. He was stoned. He and Ned surprised me even more when Ned informed me of the details of this planned party. It was to be a fetish party, and they insisted that I invite all my friends. Um . . . okay.

Matt called my cell phone the night of the party to say that "the limo" was outside. And it was a huge limo—one of those truck limos you see rappers in. Matt got out of the limo in a fluffy white fur coat and greeted me and my eight friends. (Keep in mind that all this was occurring outside of the Emerson dorms. People watching us had no idea what the fuck was going on . . . and actually, neither did we.) We got in the limo, and it headed toward South Boston.

When we arrived at Ned's, I was excited and nervous. Right away we started drinking and dancing with all these hot girls I had never seen before in my life. As we were dancing, the girls started taking off their clothes. Soon they were all naked. Without a doubt, the best party ever! What was going on?

It turned out that I had been dancing with strippers. I walked around the apartment passing all kinds of weird shit. People all in leather, girls kissing girls, a large naked man masturbating in the corner. All this was going on while Matt and all my friends were flirting and doing ecstasy. I knew they were all on the drug because they were grinding their teeth and screaming weird stuff like "Kiss me and touch my knee!"

I didn't touch anyone's knee.

As the party went on, everyone got drunker and drunker. It was absolute insanity. My girlfriend at the time was in a room hooking up with another girl who was dressed in one of Ned's costumes. Matt had apparently changed and was now dressed as a Native American with no pants. I was in a jailhouse costume with handcuffs. Everyone else was just, well, naked.

Downstairs, I found a live S&M show being taped in front of about thirty people. The show was broadcast throughout the apartment on little TV screens. You could be in the bathroom taking a piss, and on the screen beside you you'd be watching a screen of someone else taking a piss. Except you were peeing in the toilet and they were peeing on another person. My friends watching the S&M scene looked at me with expressions that said, "I don't know what the fuck is going on but . . . I love you."

I then walked into another room where a girl I recognized was drawing latex tattoos on people's nipples. I don't remember getting one, but I woke up the next day with a plastic flower on my nipple and I've seen several pictures, so I guess it happened.

Since my girlfriend was with another girl, I figured why not me. So I started kissing everyone I found hot. It was a fetish party. I had to hook up.

I believe I even kissed a girl while she was vomiting: salty, but still awesome. I woke up in the morning in a cage holding a stiletto boot. Matt was rushing out of the apartment still high on ecstasy. He was late for a children's birthday party. I moved a strange girl out of my inner thigh, pushed the sex swings aside, tripped over a bong, and left.

Outside there was no limo waiting for me. In fact, there wasn't even a taxi. As I began to walk to the T, I passed the fat, naked, masturbating guy from before, only now he had on a jump suit and a headband and was jogging. When he ran by, it occurred to me that what I had experienced the night before was exactly the kind of expression necessary to evolution.

—Emerson College

Alumni Update: The author, Dan Levy, won the title "Funniest College Comedian in America" at HBO's 2001 U.S. Comedy Arts Festival. Since then, Dan has hosted two series on MTV, *Your Face or Mine* and *The Reality Show*. Dan also wrote, produced, and starred in the television pilot *Almost Funny*, which was chosen as an official selection for the New York Television Festival. Most recently Dan is writing and hosting *The Green Room with Dan Levy*, a comedy talk show for cbs.com. Visit danlevyshow.com for more information.

LESSON LEARNED: Don't be afraid to go with the flow, even if that flow runs into a fat guy whacking off. A side lesson is not to party with magicians—and that also goes for clowns, mimes, and guys decorated with metallic paint and acting like robots.

CHAPTER 15

Beyond the Lamp Shade

A Review of Party Fouls and Social Missteps

Yes, a college party is inherently out of control. Windows are broken, speakers are blown, pants are lost. But as with most things on campus, there's an unwritten code of conduct—a sort of method to the madness. And an infraction of these rules comes in the form of the dreaded "party foul."

Savvy students learn how to walk the fine line between working the crowd and horking on the crowd; between raising the roof and punching the wall; between . . . well, you get the picture. Unfortunately, many students often step over this line on their way to taking a dump in the washing machine. Of course, what they lose in dignity, friendships, and permission to return to the state, they make up for in permanently ingrained lessons on social blunders and how to avoid them.

We hope you enjoy these egregious party errors and will use them to check your own track record.

Plenty of Party Fouls

I had just hooked up with Eric, who had been a good friend for a while. Our second date was a party at his friend's apartment. I was a little nervous, realizing that his friends would be checking out his "new girl."

Things started out fine, until Eric poured me a couple of rum and Cokes (mostly rum), and I quickly became very inebriated. When the police began pounding on the door to break up the party a couple of hours after our arrival, Eric led me into a bedroom to hide. We sat there quietly, looking out the window, and then I stretched out my legs and somehow got my foot caught up in an electrical cord. The next thing I knew, this huge lamp had crashed down onto Eric with a loud thud, and suddenly there was blood everywhere.

Drunk as I was, I laughed hysterically while Eric frantically tried to pick up the broken glass. "Ohhh," he groaned, "it's not fixable, and I think it might have been an antique!"

I got up, suddenly appreciating how serious a situation this might be—and promptly proceeded to knock over a plant! Dirt flew everywhere. Eric groaned again and left for the bathroom to put something on his bloody ear.

I was sure the girl whose room I had demolished was going to kill me. I followed Eric to the bathroom, where he was standing holding back the long, greasy hair of—yep, you guessed it—the girl whose room I just destroyed. She had overindulged as well and was heaving into the toilet.

> To repair an ear laceration, the anatomic landmarks must be lined up to prevent contour deformities—known outside the medical world as "hammer ear."

One of Eric's hands was holding the girl's hair, while the other was holding a tissue to his ear. I reached over to help hold the tissue to his ear. It was a perfect opportunity for redemption, both with Eric and the girl whose bedroom I had just inadvertently trashed. But as he took his hand off the tissue, I lost my balance and bumped into him hard, which caused him to slam the girl's head into the toilet! She came up from the water sputtering, and Eric turned to me with a disapproving glare that might have killed lesser women.

I took the hint and left. I walked to my dorm by myself, stumbling and giggling all the way. What a way to start a new relationship!

—*University of Wisconsin—Eau Claire*

Alumni Update: "Eric and I continued dating for about four months, but I broke it off since there was no 'chemistry' between us. We've remained good friends but went our separate ways for graduate school this past year. I met up with him about a month ago, and he revealed to me that he's gay—so all's well that ends well. By the way, he still has a scar on his ear."

LESSON LEARNED: Resilience will serve you well in life. Sure, you've committed not just one party foul or even two, but have assaulted your hookup, trashed someone's room, and then, through a Rube Goldberg chain of events, given a girl a power swirlie. And you can still laugh it off. That's courage—or drunkenness.

Fun on Pee Hill

I transferred to St. Joe's the second semester of freshman year. Not knowing many people yet, I decided to road trip to Shippensburg to visit my best friend, Susie. Any of you who are not familiar with the school need to make a road trip there—it is, without a doubt, the craziest school in Pennsylvania. With our supply of vodka and lemonade, we were ready to get utterly retarded.

Sufficiently lubricated, we ventured down a path through the woods (goat path) toward frat row. Considering that we were tipsy, it was nearly impossible to traverse that dirt hill in the pitch dark. We found our way in a most unexpected fashion . . .

Susie squatted down and took a piss in the woods and, in the steam that rose up from her pee, we saw the reflection of a spotlight from one of the frat houses. Having found our way, we pounded what was left of our vodka and lemonade, and headed to the party.

Under typical conditions, human urine has a temperature between 90 and 100 degrees.

The frat house was pretty packed. But Susie and I still quickly found our way to the keg. The beer was going down really well. We felt unstoppable.

After a good amount of beer, I decided to break the seal. The line for the bathroom was way too long, and I thought I was going to pee my pants. Someone nearby told me that we could pee outside behind this fence, that "the guys do it all the time." Being drunk and silly, I decided that this was a great idea. So, I grabbed Susie and we headed outside.

It was late in the night, and let's just say that a lot of other people had already taken advantage of the hill, so it was quite slippery. I carefully positioned myself next to the fence and pulled down my pants. As soon as I squatted down, my feet began to slip. Luckily (for me), I grabbed onto the fence and caught myself.

Susie wasn't so lucky.

She tumbled all the way down the hill, her ass glowing in the moonlight, and ended up in the woods. As I turned to watch her slide, I couldn't help myself, and I began laughing hysterically. And so did Susie! (If she had been in the right state of mind, she would have been worrying about all the funky diseases she was probably contracting.) When I looked back up the hill toward the house, I saw what seemed like half the frat outside taking pictures of us!

> The original master of the pratfall, comedian Chevy Chase, attended Bard College in Annandale-on-Hudson, New York. There is no word if they, too, had a pee hill.

The two of us got up that hill as fast as we could and headed home. I'm sure that's when the frat guys got some of the best photos: the two of us doing our best to run up that pee-soaked hill, trying to pull our pants up as we ran, and Susie covered head to toe in mud and piss.

The next time I came out to visit her, I made sure that I didn't venture out to "pee hill," as we like to call it. What crazy times at Shippensburg!

—*St. Joe's University*

LESSON LEARNED: Urination is no time to start exploring the road less traveled. As we've seen, that path can quickly become the sight of a colossal—and messy—party foul.

Getting Tanked with the Stars

The story you are about to read is true. The names have been changed to protect my college buddy, who vomited all over a pop star's house.

A few days before New Year's Eve 2004, I miraculously ended up invited to a party in the Hollywood Hills. I shouldn't say whose house it was because if he reads this, we will *never* be invited back. I will say this—he's in a boy band, and not one of those pretend boy bands like 98° or O-Town or the Jackson Five.

> Winona Ryder, while still hot, was convicted in 2002 of felony grand theft and vandalism for stealing several thousand dollars worth of merchandise from a store.

A friend of a friend knew the guy, so I somehow ended up on the guest list. There were about one hundred people there. A bunch of people from all those Fox and WB coming-of-age sitcoms, some dude from *The Sandlot,* half of one of those other boy bands (oh no! drama!), and some random actors I didn't recognize. Allegedly, Winona Ryder was there, but I don't believe it because my jacket was still in the closet after she left. But who came to the party is not important. What's important is how often my friend threw up.

My friend John had been talking to a girl for an hour and a half before she mentioned her boyfriend. *An hour and a half.* There are two party fouls girls with boyfriends are guilty of. Mentioning the boyfriend after being arm in arm with someone for *an hour and a half,* or mentioning the boyfriend way too early. I prefer the second one, and I'm sure John would have, too. Though that can also be annoying:

"So, where you from?"

"I'm from Indiana. And so is my boyfriend."

When the girl dropped the "boyfriend" bomb, John had had a little too much to drink. And then he did, like, eight more shots. So when it was time for us to say, "Bye Bye Bye," I discovered John passed out on the cooler outside. John is six foot seven. While I dragged him indoors, he came *very* close to falling in the pool. I contemplated letting him do so just for the story, but I managed to get him through the house and down to the street, all while calling a cab.

The thing you need to understand about houses in the Hollywood Hills is that the driveways are about three blocks long and steeper than most of San Francisco. Stumbling, falling, and yelling, "Don't control me!" John made getting him down to the street a remarkable accomplishment.

Our cab came, but someone else nabbed it while I was trying to keep John from dying. We called a few more cabs and other people took those, too. Then another one clearly came for us, and someone took that. I shouldn't tell you who did it, but it would have been awesome if as he stole my cab, he said, "Welcome to *The O.C.*!"

While we waited another hour to be picked up, John lay there on the red-brick walk, completely passed out. The final vomit count was five—once in each bathroom, once on the lawn, once over the railing, and once just lying on the ground. So I did what anyone in my situation would have done—I took a picture with my new camera phone so I'd have proof. Maybe I should tell Sprint so they can use the story in their next commercial.

And that really sums me up—it's my first big Hollywood party, and one of my college buddies pukes all over a pop star's house. Oh man. I can't wait to see this episode of *MTV Cribs*.

—*Columbia University*

Alumni Update: Steve Hofstetter is a nationally touring comedian, a host on Sirius Satellite Radio, and a columnist for *Sports Illustrated*. He is also the author of the *Student Body Shots* series. His work and tour dates can be found on SteveHofstetter.com.

LESSON LEARNED: Here's an example of how a college party foul is even more dangerous in the "real world." Outside the context of everyone passing out and puking up, it sticks out like a sore thumb—a sore, passed out, and puking-up thumb, that is.

Falling for Claire Danes

If you look at the career paths of certain actors, you might notice gaps of a year or two in their work. The reasons for this are myriad: marriage, children, traveling, burnout, whatever.

Take Claire Danes, for instance. From 1999 to 2002, you won't find her name attached to any films. The commonly accepted reason for this was her time spent as a student at Yale University. But I know the real reason: I scared her out of show business for three years.

> Claire Danes did not appear in any movies between *The Mod Squad* and *Brokedown Palace* in 1999 and *Igby Goes Down* and *The Hours* in 2002.

It was 1999, the last year UConn and Yale played each other in football. And I remember part of that day pretty well. I was up at 6:00 A.M. to start drinking; I had to be sure I was wrecked by the time we got to New Haven at 8:00 A.M. After all, we had only four hours of tailgating before the game started, at noon. And then, we didn't even go into the Yale Bowl for the game; we just kept drinking outside the stadium.

My friend Norah drove us (in my car) down to New Haven, with a keg in the trunk and a gleam in our eyes. We got to the stadium, and there they were: busloads of UConn Greeks, rows of kegs, and a sea of Husky blue. We were in for a great time.

We set up our keg next to a friend's and downed beer after beer as the morning sun glistened over Long Island Sound. Then things got weird. The last thing I remembered was funneling a beer, and then I woke up in a school bus. Couples were in various stages of undress around me, yet I was totally clothed and stuffed in the backseat. Confused, I got up and walked off the bus, careful not to disturb the couple having sex in front of me.

I looked around for my savior. "Norah! Norah! Where are you?"

Some dude said, "She's gone, man. She got drunk and left."

I had never seen this man before in my life, yet strangely I believed him. So I trudged off toward a nice set of trees, hungry for shade and a moment to stretch out.

And then it happened. While sitting against a tree, sucking down two beers, I saw three girls walking past me—and the one in the middle was her, Claire Danes. The blond hair. The piercing eyes. And that body. Oh, man, was she hot.

So I started to stand up. I called out to her, "Hey! Aren't you Claire Danes?"

She turned around as if in slow motion. "Yes, I am," she replied.

Claire's letter of recommendation to Yale University was written by director Oliver Stone, which totally beats yours.

"You were so cool in *My So-Called Life*!" I bellowed.

She blushed. "Umm . . . thanks."

Now, I could have stopped there, and things would've been fine. But no, I *had* to try to walk toward her, drunk as hell. "Hey, are you in any movies . . ."

BAM! I tripped over myself and fell face-first on the ground, right in front of her. All six feet seven inches of me. The girls jumped back, shocked and horrified that such a huge human being had just crashed to the ground in front of them. I pulled myself up, slowly. They backed away from me, honestly scared, and then ran away.

I stood there for about ten minutes, half out of shock and half because I had forgotten how to walk. The thought was burning in my head: *I almost crushed Claire Danes.*

It's been years since then. I've gone on to get a master's degree, and Claire has gone on to act in some of Hollywood's biggest flicks. But until the day I die, I will remain convinced that her three-year hiatus was because a tall undergrad almost crushed her in a drunken stupor.

—*University of Connecticut*

Alumni Update: The tall drunken fool was Marty Lang, who, after graduating from UConn, wrote for the *New York Times.* He also produced three independent films before earning a Master of Fine Arts degree at the Florida State University Film Conservatory. A film he produced, *The Plunge,* won a 2004 Student Academy Award. He is now a filmmaker and college professor in Connecticut.

LESSON LEARNED: This is a lesson in opportunism. If you can commit a party foul in front of someone way more famous than you, go for it. The story of pulling a Chris Farley in front of one of our generation's finest actresses is something to share with the grandkids.

CHAPTER 16

Dead to the World

Exploring the Inappropriate Pass-Out

The old adage of campus life holds true: "Rules, and freshman lofts, are made to be broken." But sometimes, the human body, like a professor fighting for tenure, is a little harder to break, especially when it comes to how much booze your body can handle. When that limit is reached, your faculties and consciousness take their bat and ball and head home. Welcome to the demented world of the pass-out.

Now we can't get up on a soapbox and tell you not to drink. One reason being: Who stands on soapboxes anymore? But we do need to mention that passing out is a sign you've had way too much. The pass-out can be your body's best teaching aid. It drives the point home, especially when you wake up in a different country with a suitcase full of pinecones. Sure, pass-out stories such as the ones to follow are funny, but they also offer a valuable lesson: if you push your limits, you better learn from them for the next time.

Remember one last important rule: Know when to say . . . hey, wake up. Somebody help me get him up to bed!

Chicken Driven Wild

Michigan State becomes a veritable Mardi Gras on Halloween. All over campus, frat boys dressed as Chippendale dancers get frisked by "police officers" in miniskirts, while superheroes and cartoon characters play beer pong and stagger the streets in profound drunken harmony.

One Halloween was particularly eventful for an acquaintance of mine named Jake. Jake was so wasted after an evening of indulgence that he mistook the Spartan City for his home campus of Eastern Michigan U, and foolishly decided that he should attempt to navigate the labyrinthine streets until he found his apartment complex. After a few hours of wobbling down sidewalk/lawn/street/sidewalk, Jake realized that he was freezing, and he got into an unlocked vehicle to warm up.

After passing in and out of consciousness, he awoke amazed to find himself behind the wheel. This mysterious occurrence led him to the conclusion that he should simply drive to his apartment, as it would be warmer and much faster. (Warning: do *not* attempt this, folks.)

Wal-Mart pulled copies of *Grand Theft Auto: San Andreas* off store shelves because of the game's hard-core content.

Of course, the fabulously observant East Lansing Police pulled Jake over, but it was only in part due to the fact that the vehicle was weaving like an old spinster. Are you wondering why said vehicle was unlocked and had the keys in the ignition? As it turns out, the vehicle that Jake clambered into was an ambulance. Jake was promptly arrested for grand theft auto and whatever the charge is for stealing an ambulance.

The only thing that could make this drunken spectacle more hilarious was Jake's ironic choice of cos-

In 2004, a man wearing a chicken suit robbed a grocery store in Columbus, Ohio.

tume: all of the night's events he performed were from the feathered depths of a giant chicken outfit. I'll leave the cross-the-road jokes to your discretion.

As far as I know, Jake pled guilty to all charges and was dismissed with minimal punishment by a judge who declared his actions not so much criminal as really, really stupid.

—*Michigan State University*

LESSON LEARNED: Nothing good is going to happen when you get behind the wheel when you're drunk—even if you're not planning to drive. An equally important lesson is when dressed as a chicken, maybe you should practice a modicum of moderation.

Puff Puff Pass-Out

My roomie and I were invited to hang with some of the degenerates who attend the local community college way out in BFE. Not being a student at the community college, I knew no one there. My roomie, however, had grown up with several of them. After cursory introductions to a couple of very drunk ballplayers, my roomie immediately took off with her cutie for the night.

> BFE: Short for Bum Fucking Egypt. Describes some place far out of the way.

As the lone Baylor student, I was considered by everyone to be a snob, and no one talked to me. It wouldn't have been so bad if I could have resorted to the bottle to end the boredom. But, the *hosts* had consumed all of the booze before we got there. I made awkward conversation with a few guys as we watched a *Dukes of Hazzard* rerun. When the opportunity arose to have a little bud with some stoners who had stumbled into the party, I readily accepted.

> Ben Jones, aka Cooter from *The Dukes of Hazzard,* was elected to the United States House of Representatives from the Fourth District of Georgia.

I happily stood on the back porch with these guys, taking a couple of hits and laughing about the people inside. Now, I am not one of those chicks who are on their ass after taking one toke—not by any means. To this day, I maintain that whatever I smoked that night was not straight marijuana.

After the sixth, maybe seventh hit, I was out. I mean, that was it. I don't remember anything save one small detail: I could not feel my body at all, which someone had placed in a lawn chair.

The next morning, I awoke locked in the trunk of my car. Yeah. The trunk. I pushed down the backseat and crawled through the trunk hatch, my feet strangely heavy. Once out, I realized the reason: I had on Rollerblades. I still don't know why. But I had all my clothes on, which is always reassuring. The ground outside my car was drenched—do I have to say with what? I was still queasy and my vision was extremely blurred. I was more disoriented than I can ever remember being—this from a girl who never has hangovers.

When I angrily asked my roommate what the hell had happened the night before, she told me that no one had seen me since I left the party for a smoke. No one had any idea who the stoners were. She had figured I was still around because my car was still there. Yeah, with me passed out in the trunk!

> The Federal Motor Carrier Safety Administration 571.401 Standard No. 401 establishes the requirement for providing a trunk-release mechanism that makes it possible for a person trapped inside a trunk to escape.

These days I'm much more careful about whom I smoke out with, and I no longer hang out with community college kids. By the way, if anyone wants to fill me in on what the hell I smoked that night, I'd sure appreciate it.

—*Baylor University*

LESSON LEARNED: Looks like you've already learned those two important lessons in life everyone needs to learn: Watch out who you smoke with, and don't hang with community college kids. Except those community college kids who own a copy of this book or who have really good pot.

Easter Resurrection

My longtime girlfriend was going out of town Easter weekend, and my best friend, the youngest of all my friends, was turning twenty-one. Normally I would hang out with my friends for a while and then spend time with my girlfriend. But since she was out of town and it was Joey's twenty-first, I vowed to stay out all night long.

I dropped my girlfriend off at the airport Saturday evening and went straight to my friend's house. We started with the usual pre-gaming: beer pong, asshole, etc. Then we went to Bourbon Street and hung out at Pat O'Brien's for about four hours. By 2:00 A.M., when we left, we were all really drunk. When we got to F&M's Bar, Joey and Tony got out of the cab and went to take a leak. Unfortunately, a cop drove by just then and arrested them both for public urination.

Keep in mind, it was now early Easter Sunday morning. As the cops were booking our friends, I tried (and failed) to bribe them with the seven sweaty singles I had in my back pocket. They shrugged me off, but my friend Kelly began yelling at them. "Oh, when my house is broken into it takes you guys four hours to get there, but when my friend is peeing outside on his birthday, you guys are right there!"

> The official fine for public urination is up to five hundred dollars or ninety days in jail. The unofficial penalty, which some sadistic cops have been known to levy, is a round of push-ups in the puddle you've just made on the sidewalk.

Surprisingly, her argument failed to sway the police, and the cops took Joey and Tony away. My other friends all went to call a cab so they could bail them out of jail, but I started to go into the bar, telling them, "C'mon guys, let's go. Drinks are on me." They told me they were going home, and I just said, "I'll be at the bar," not realizing, I think, that they were leaving.

I sat down at the bar, opened a tab, and proceeded to forget the next four or five hours of my life. When I next became conscious of where I was, I found myself shivering and soaked on a porch in Metairie—some forty minutes outside of New Orleans—playing with some little kid's toys at 9:00 A.M., Easter Sunday morning, and wearing one flip-flop.

I had no idea how I got there, only that I wanted to play with this little kid's toys. A cop car pulled up to the house and a cop got out and said to me, "You know, you can't be doing this," to which I incoherently mumbled, "I live on Palmer and Willow. I live on Palmer and Willow," over and over again. The cop sighed (I think—I don't really remember) and put me in the back of his car.

I felt bad for the family who lived there; they'd probably left their house to go to church on Easter Sunday and found a rain-soaked wacko on their front porch! Anyway, as the cops were driving me back to my house, my phone (which I thankfully still had) rang. It was my friends, trying to raise bail money for Joey and Tony. Not remembering what had happened the night before, I was surprised and said, "Joey got arrested? I'll get some money. We'll bail him out!"

My friends called back two more times, and each time I was equally surprised to talk to them, to hear that Joey had been arrested, and equally ready to help bail him out.

The cops dropped me off at my house and told me to be more careful. I got into my house, dumped my pockets out on my pool table, and passed out for about eight hours. When I awoke, I realized I was missing a lot of cash, my ID, and my credit card, and that I had a receipt for "The Dock," a bar that isn't near either F&M's or Metairie.

That night I went back to F&M's on the hunch that I had left my bar tab unpaid. I discovered I had run up a hundred-dollar tab. The bar had my ID as well. The guy gave me a free beer to be nice, and as I turned to leave, I noticed something: my other flip-flop, lying in the middle of the dance floor. I picked it up and went home—ashamed to be alive.

—Tulane University

LESSON LEARNED: Binge drinking and passing out can be costly. Open tabs and lost footwear alone have made a serious dent in the economy.

From Wild Start to Finnish

First of all, you should know that at the time of these events I was living in Finland and had managed to acquire a semi-regular job with good pay, in addition to taking a full college course load. Finally, at the end of July, I had a short break.

I decided to celebrate my long-awaited freedom in the only sensible way: by going on a bender. I stocked my cellar with all the alcohol I could get my hands on, some food, and, of course, skunk. With everything ready, it was time to begin the festivities.

I invited around twenty of my best friends, who were more than willing to join in the fun. The first night went well, despite everyone being really quiet. Probably we were just too stoned to talk.

It was apparently halfway into the second day that things began spinning out of control. The alcohol binge had continued through the night, and everyone looked and felt like something out of a B-grade zombie movie. I was sent out to get more liquor, and left with my traveling suitcase to carry the booze back.

Next thing I knew, I woke up. In a bush. Halfway into my suitcase. Which was filled with pinecones.

> **Time traveling:** Used to describe blackouts that occur during drinking binges.

Clutching one pant leg—pants not belonging to me. Sufficiently weird? It gets better.

After ten minutes of cursing the ache in my head, I stumbled out of the bush wanting to know where I was. Emerging from the bush, I was greeted by the sight of Buckingham Palace.

At this point, I was sure I was still dreaming, comfortably tucked away in my bed in Oulu, Finland. But, as my headache increased, I had to admit that I was wide awake. In London. With a huge headache. And a suitcase full of pinecones. Looking like a bag of walking camel shit.

Wanting to clear my head a bit, I headed, via an ATM, to a nearby market/kiosk to buy beer. With the aid of my beer, I started my ascent to reality by checking my wallet. I found a train ticket from Oulu (my hometown) to Helsinki (Finland's capital) and a plane ticket stub from Helsinki to London. Also, searching through my case of pinecones, I found my passport, which I had obviously left in there and then found on my beer run.

Oulu is the site of the Annual Air Guitar World Championship.

Having downed several beers by now, I found the situation funnier by the minute. The biggest upside? I was in London! I decided to make the best of it, so I headed to Camden, which, in my experience, is the easiest place in London to get skunk. And within ten minutes of getting to Camden, I was once again adequately supplied to get wasted.

After more than enough beer and skunk, one of those 3-D movies and another night in a bush with my suitcase, I realized it was about time to get home. Not wanting to fly back, I decided to go through Europe by train.

So, I hopped on a train from London to Lille, completely (well, at least somewhat) sober, and began the wait. A group of twenty-somethings were sitting near me, and they kept staring at me, probably amused by my appearance, permanently glazed eyes and all.

After some conversation, they said they were planning on going to Amsterdam, and asked whether I'd come along. Figuring I could get back to Finland through Denmark and Sweden—and not wanting to pass on an opportunity to hang out in Amsterdam—I readily agreed.

I ended up spending two days in Amsterdam in the world's worst hostel, passing not a single sober moment in memory and having pretty much the time of my life. My new friends were the jolliest bunch of drunks I'd ever seen, and were more than eager to participate in a variety of salacious activities.

> Klaatu is a Canadian band that had five studio albums during the time they were together, 1973–1982. None of which is at any risk of being stolen.

Anyway, all good things must come to an end, and eventually I left for home, and had a very uneventful journey back, finally arriving nearly a week after I had gone out for some beer.

(I swear on my near-mint-condition original Klaatu record that this story is 100 percent true.)

—*Kuusiluodon Lukio*

LESSON LEARNED: Spontaneity can lead to some great experiences. Go with it, kill the plans, and just see where life takes you—and don't forget to pack your pinecones.

CHAPTER 17

Poopers of the Party

A Survey of That Guy and That Girl

One of the most popular mantras on campuses is "Don't Be That Guy." And by this, students mean avoiding fully transforming yourself into a Jungian doppelgänger who betrays the community's tacit social mores. Er . . . in other words, don't get drunk, put your car in a tree, and drop a deuce in your skivvies.

For those who don't know, That Guy/Girl is a living, breathing, spilling party foul—uncouth incarnate. He/she is louder than a human fire alarm, more annoying than a group project without a smart Asian kid to do the work, known to walk through screen doors in a single bound.

But that doesn't mean there's not something to be learned here. The That Guy alter ego teaches you about your repressed nature and even provides insight into your true self—assuming you can remember what this other self did in those pantyhose. For your friends, it provides lasting memories of watching their beloved suite mate attempt to fly out of the second-floor window. And for you, the reader, it offers a lesson in dealing with it all.

Enjoy the following stories. While the topics may be less Jung and more Jägermeister, you'll be better off in the long run.

Epic Party Adventure

The party was at a roommate's parents' house in a very affluent neighborhood in Roswell, Georgia. It was the perfect party house, with a hot tub, several big-screen televisions, and a huge deck. I arrived at about 7:00 P.M. and went right for the barbeque and the beer.

Around 9:00 P.M., I got into a fight with a friend's girlfriend. So, to avoid further conflict, I drove up to a local bar, where I knew the managers. Upon spotting me at the bar, one of the managers started pouring me Jägermeister shots. After about ten shots and a couple of beers, I decided that I had cooled off enough to return to the party. My vehicle at the time was a Jeep CJ7, which was a blast to drive off-road. Even though I had gone off-roading in that area several times before, this time I managed to get hung up in a tree, in front of the HoneyBaked Ham store!

I knew I would be screwed if I got caught drunk with my car in a tree, so my *brilliant plan* was to take the keys out of the ignition, toss them

> The urban legend that Jägermeister contains deer or elk blood is unfounded.

far away from my car, and run back to the party. I knew the cops would see the Jeep halfway up a tree and immediately try to find the driver. Therefore, the woods behind the neighborhood seemed like a safer path than running along the road.

I started running through the woods GI Joe style. And in my drunken state I shouldn't have been surprised that I fell a couple of times, getting

> Sneaky drunk: An individual who, when drunk, has an increased sense of stealth and cunning. This individual often suffers from delusions of invisibility.

wet and covered with briers. Quickly my clothes were soaked, and I was itching like crazy.

After several more minutes, I figured I should be close to the house, so I ran out onto the nearest street. Sure enough, I was on the right cul-de-sac. I decided to enter the house "stealth mode" from the rear by walking up the deck stairs. I noticed that all the lights were out. But it had gotten pretty late, so I assumed that everyone had simply passed out for the night. I found the back door unlocked. I entered and immediately went for the refrigerator. I noticed a change in the way the fridge looked, but I chalked this up to my drunken state. I opened up the freezer to see if they had any food. Hot dogs!

I put the package on the counter and grabbed a knife from the drawer. Before I went to work on the dogs, I became distracted by how uncomfortable my wet and itchy clothes were. Thinking nothing of it, I stripped down to my boxers. Feeling better without my nasty clothes, I set my attention to my feast. The hot dogs were hard to pry apart from one another, so I began on them with the knife. Before I had made much progress, I noticed a figure standing in the entryway to the kitchen.

I briefly glanced up to see a short, stocky thirty-something guy standing in the shadows in the connecting family room. As I stood there, clad only in my flannel boxers, he glared at me through sleepy eyes, his face red as a beet. "What *the hell* are you doing?"

I replied curtly, "I'm cooking up some food and waiting on Bud (the host of the party). What the hell are you doing?"

The man's red face started to contort into an almost indescribable shape, straining every single one of his facial muscles in an expression of anger. Then he took off.

I shook off the incident and decided to look for some other kind of food, because the hot dogs were too much work. There were some pizza rolls in the freezer, which I threw into the microwave. They took about ten minutes to cook, and they smelled great as the ringer went off. Just as I picked up the plate of rolls, I heard a husky voice say, "Drop them." I turned around to find no fewer than five police officers standing there, all with their weapons drawn. It was a pretty sobering scene to be standing there in my boxers facing five cops, their guns gleaming in the light.

In 1968, Jeno Paulucci invented the first pizza roll using an old egg roll machine.

"Drop what?" I asked. "The pizza rolls?"

The cop closest to me grabbed the plate and threw me up against the oven repeatedly. I figured they had found my Jeep and tracked me back to Bud's kitchen. They were asking questions about why I was there, and all I kept saying was, "Okay, you found me. Okay." During that sobering beatdown, I also started to realize that something about the house was not right. Then it hit me: I was in the wrong house. The cops didn't want to hear about it as they took me out to the squad car in the driveway. I desperately tried to explain that the house I was supposed to be at was next door, and it was a simple mix-up. Finally, the cops escorted me over to Bud's house. Luckily, Bud came to the door—even though, as I later found out, he had been about to have sex with one of the hotter chicks at the party when the cops knocked. (God bless you, Bud.)

Bud confirmed that, indeed, he did know me, and that I was at his house that night. Thankfully, the cops released me.

A couple of hours later, however, the cops returned to Bud's house. Ironically, they had gone to the HoneyBaked Ham parking lot to fill out the report of my trespass. They saw the Jeep up in the tree, ran the plates, and now they demanded an explanation from me.

I threw up my hands in amazement, "You found it. Someone stole my Jeep earlier tonight, thank you so much!" The cop simply laughed and closed his ticket book. He said he wasn't going to give me a DUI if I admitted to having driven it. So, I copped the plea bargain.

In the morning I went to apologize to the family that I had so rudely awakened the previous night. When I rang the doorbell, this beautiful blond housewife with her two-year-old came to the door.

Apparently, the night before, her husband had gone straight for his gun, and it was all she and the cops could do to keep him from going downstairs and shooting me. He was still so pissed that he refused to come to the door to hear my apology.

"One more thing," she said, "did you at least get to eat some of our hot dogs? You left them all over my new kitchen floor."

Oops.

—*Georgia State University*

LESSON LEARNED: When your That Guy alter ego can escape death so many times—and score free hot dogs—you need to wonder what the hell your sober self brings to the party.

The Pantyhose Nightmare

Life in a University of Maryland fraternity has more than its share of stereotypical and clichéd college moments. The intermittent camaraderie is nice, and I still have a handful of great friends from those years. But one night toward the end of my junior year made my four-hundred-dollar-per-semester dues worth every penny.

Among all the things you see in the movies that give fraternities a bad name is "The Formal." Twice a year, a bunch of overconfident beer chuggers don their only suits and ties and head to a ballroom for a "classy evening." You know the drill:

> In spring 2004, both the fraternity and sorority grade point averages at the University of Maryland were higher than that of the university population at large.

a DJ, a handful of white-clothed and candlelit tables strewn about, a dance floor in the middle, and a buffet with wings, mozzarella sticks, and maybe some salad for the sorority gals.

The first hour is standard fare for any formal gathering, in college or not: a never-ending line of people waiting for drinks at the bar and complaining about how the bar should have ten bartenders. The ladies visit the bathroom in droves to check their hair and gossip about the guys.

During the second hour, everyone is two-fisting drinks, laughing about how goofy the other campus organizations are, and talking about the professors for the 100-level classes.

The start of the third hour is when people finally notice the dance floor, and the drunken horde begins treating the ballroom like any number of the campus's not-so-sanitary establishments that serve cheap beer to underage students.

Nobody is dancing on the tables (yet), but the songs are the same cheesy dance tunes you hear at every bar, and some of the guys have their ties around their heads. Half of the women have left their dates to chat in a corner, and the guys don't even seem to be bothered by this.

The last hour is when it all happens. Three fourths of this crew is drunk, including a few who are completely blitzed out of their minds.

One of these was Margaret, a pretty average sorority girl, at least up until this point in her collegiate career. Margaret went in for what seemed like her sixteenth trip to the bathroom, after probably just as many drinks. Many college girls aren't used to wearing pantyhose on a daily basis, so "The Formal" presents an extra challenge for them, especially while drunk. Most still remember them when going to the bathroom, but there are always a few tipsy women who accidentally tuck their skirt into the waistband of their hose—or worse.

Much worse.

Our damsel in distress came stumbling out of the restroom with a relieved look on her face. Her skirt was fine, not accidentally tucked in. Her shoe bottoms were free of TP. Her hair and makeup were okay. She was only a little sweaty. I wasn't pay-

> In 1959, Glen Raven Mills of North Carolina introduced pantyhose—underpants and stockings all in one garment.

ing full attention, but I could spot a group of people when they smelled shit. It was a process. It started with the sniffing and the scrunched expressions. The accusations followed, then the pointing, and finally the howling laughter. Our dear inebriated Margaret had taken a dump but had forgotten to pull down her pantyhose.

I'll let that sink in . . .

She'd dropped a bomb in her tights. Now, oozing out of the small holes in her pantyhose, up and down her legs, was poo. It began to collect a bit around her ankles, almost like fresh chocolate doughnuts. You think she would've noticed an unusually clean wipe, but I guess she thought she was just having a good day. Your own mind can now take over envisioning the ensuing bedlam.

Fraternity dues worth every penny. Incredible thing to witness. We never saw Margaret again.

—*University of Maryland*

LESSON LEARNED: Don't be That Girl at big functions. Backing out the brown trout in your drawers in front of all your peers makes a great visual for an anti-drinking campaign. Possibly the most startling image since Nick Nolte's mug shot.

Acid Trip

Ecstasy, I recently learned, was originally invented as an appetite suppressant by Merck Pharmaceuticals in the 1920s. I was never overweight,

> Ecstasy (MDMA) was patented in 1912 to be used in the manufacturing of styptic pencils. It was more than fifty years before someone ingested it and had a killer party.

but I did take Merck's appetite suppressant when I went to visit Brown University as a high school senior trying to figure out where to go to college. Damn, that was a great visit. Brown should give out ecstasy to all prospective applicants.

I couldn't believe how wonderful everything at the school was. "I love this cafeteria!" I thought to myself. "This is the most beautiful cafeteria I've ever seen. And this baked ziti—this is freakin' delicious! You get to live in *these* dorm rooms? They're palaces! And your library carrels are so well designed. What beautiful fluorescent lighting! God, look at that pile of bricks in the yard. That's the most gorgeous pile of bricks at any college I've ever seen."

I think I gave out about fifteen hugs to surprised and apprehensive students who had made the mistake of wandering within a twenty-foot radius of me.

Unfortunately, the ecstasy had worn off by the time I actually became a freshman at Brown and learned that the baked ziti actually tasted like Styrofoam dipped in ketchup.

—*Brown University*

Alumni Update: A. J. Jacobs studied Philosophy at Brown University. He worked for the *Antioch Daily Ledger* and *Entertainment Weekly* before becoming an *Esquire* magazine editor. He has authored several books, including *The Know-It-All: One Man's Humble Quest to Become the Smartest Person in the World, The Two Kings: Elvis and Jesus, America Off-Line: The Complete Outernet Starter,* and his newest, *A Year of Living Biblical.*

LESSON LEARNED: If you have the That Guy gene, then you might as well let everyone know as soon as you enroll in school—if not before.

That Girl Who Could Fly

I remember it as if it were last week, but it was actually last September— during my freshman year at the University of North Florida. That Friday night we were throwing a huge party to celebrate my friend Rich's twenty-first birthday. We got four kegs, made about 450 Jell-O shots, and bought tons and tons of liquor for what would later be referred to simply as "*the* party of the year."

As the night progressed, I proceeded to drink and drink and drink—so I was already pretty wasted when my friend D-Rock decided to challenge me to a Jell-O shot contest. Sure, it sounds fun until you look at the stats:

D-Rock is three hundred pounds and almost six feet tall. I, on the other hand, am one hundred five pounds and only five feet three inches tall. He was up to forty-six shots while I was still around twenty-four, yet I was determined to win. However, I managed to get only one more down before my friend Rich dragged me out of the kitchen and onto the couch, where he forbade me to ingest even one more ounce of alcohol.

I had not been on the couch for more than five or ten minutes when my roommate, Emily, started yelling that the cops had arrived and we needed to flee before we were "sent to prison forever!"

We ran upstairs and ducked into one of the bedrooms. We locked the door behind us in a desperate attempt to buy some time. Emily thought we should hide under the bed; however, I thought it would be better to jump out the window. I had already begun evaluating the fall.

In my drunken haze, it didn't seem too long a fall (we were *only* on the second floor). And to further entice us, there just happened to be a futon mattress on the ground that Rich had thrown out earlier that day. From our vantage point, the futon appeared to be lying directly beneath the window. "Score!" I thought to myself.

So, we made a pact to jump. I would go first, and Emily would follow. I backed up a couple of steps, then took a running jump out the window. As I was flying through the air, it occurred to me that maybe I was actually *flying*. (Yes, I was that drunk.) About two tenths of a second later, however, I knew I was not flying, but falling, and fast. I landed flat on my ass on the hard cement. I had totally missed the futon mattress. My legs looked helpless sticking straight out in front of me. I tried to stand up, but to no avail as my legs wobbled underneath me and I promptly fell back down.

Base-jumper Adrian Nicholas holds the record for the longest unassisted human flight, at 4.55 minutes.

Emily was convinced that the cops would still be able to see me if I was sprawled out on the ground. So I began to slither into the bushes just behind the apartment building, dragging my legs behind me. Mud-soaked, I lay in the bushes for what felt like an eternity, but in reality was probably only about ten minutes. Emily started to become hysterical over my disappearance. She ran downstairs telling everyone at the entire party that I had just flung myself out a window and that I was "probably dead." It turned out that the cops were never actually there.

Another famous fly woman, Amelia Earhart, enrolled at Columbia University to study premed but quit after just one year.

Rich and a couple other guys came out to find me. They picked me up in my half-conscious state and threw me in the shower. After I got cleaned up, Stan (a guy I was seeing at the time who also lived there) brought me one of his big T-shirts, carried me back upstairs, and put me to bed. He *had* to carry me because I couldn't walk; one of my heels and my back were in extreme pain.

Even after all I had been through, Stan *still* wanted to get it on. I could barely move, my back hurt so bad, and he was asking me to get it on! The nerve! Eventually, we both passed out.

And that is how I became known as "that girl who jumped out the window."

Needless to say, the next night I stayed in and watched movies!

—*University of North Florida*

LESSON LEARNED: While your That Girl personality may defy social convention and sometimes even the law, gravity affects all of your personalities. Physics—the great equalizer of drunk people.

TRAVEL

Ah, the college road trip.
What better way to spread beer-fueled mayhem?
—Homer Simpson

The travel tale is a particularly interesting element of the college story and ranges from international intrigue to odysseys for munchies—and everything in between.

What makes the travel tale especially interesting, though, is that it gives us a glimpse of the student outside of the campus's protective coating. Gone are the free shuttles and free meal plans and free incompetent medical services.

Our post-pubescent heroes and heroines in these stories must fend for themselves during these voyages into the outside world. Some succeed—finding that their newly acquired bravado and creativity are more than the rest of the townie world can handle. Others don't fare as well—finding that the real world and its rules are too lame or too sober.

Either way, these travelers are like hunters—fearless (and penniless) souls in search of the next great experience. While the hunt is fun, the best part is bringing the kill back to the tribe, retelling the exploits to your wide-eyed tribe/suite mates. Giving them a little taste of the meat—but keeping the succulent snout as a treat for yourself.

Okay, our metaphor broke down, but the point remains: The best part of wild college journeys is sharing the stories. And while you most likely don't know these people (unless one of them saw your mom's knockers), we hope you feel like you're part of their post-hunt celebration.

So grab a futon and a femur, and join us for these tales of collegiate travels.

CHAPTER 18

The Stink from the Backseat

A Tribute to the Road Trip

The American road trip is a time-honored tradition. It's the stuff forever preserved for generations with photos in scrapbooks, shoe boxes of ticket stubs, and scars along the buttock region.

Inherent in every road trip is a quest for something—something outside the campus cocoon. Whether it's a concert, a sporting event, or simply a place to party (and then trash) without repercussions, something treasured must lurk at the end of the voyage.

Thus the collegiate traveler embarks on a journey—one that is part Homer Simpson and part that other Homer, the old Greek dude who wrote that poem—and brings back these tales of places unseen and incidents previously undocumented. And through these tales, the college traveler demonstrates how to make critical decisions, such as how to grab breakfast six states away, how to think on your feet, especially when you don't have a floor to stand on, and ultimately how to face new places and new challenges without getting all *Rainman.*

So join us on these trips that take us out of the ordinary and into whole new worlds—and new places to drink.

The Munchies Mecca

It was a cold Sunday afternoon in Cortland, New York (about thirty miles south of Syracuse). My five roommates and I were having one of those standard college conversations—entertaining but of little substance. This particular conversation was centered on the "Greatest Places We've Ever Eaten"—pretty deep stuff, I know. We were going to a state school, so we weren't supposed to be worried about academics anyway.

As we were talking, a roommate (Jeff "Lerm" Lemeire) and I agreed that the best place either of us had ever had breakfast was at a buffet in Myrtle Beach, South Carolina, called the Sea Mist. We had both been there during our adolescent and high school years. The restaurant's menu was unparalleled: from made-to-order waffles to just about anything you could ever want.

> The Sea Mist Oceanfront Resort's famous breakfast buffet is served at Tena's Restaurant, named after Tena Ammons, one of the founders of the resort.

At about 6:00 P.M., during our intramural volleyball game, the conversation continued and I suggested that we head out after the game to make it for breakfast at the Sea Mist the following morning. At the completion of the game, I continued to push Lerm, and finally he agreed.

We were going to travel twelve hours for breakfast.

We attempted to corral others, but people either didn't believe we were going, had some bullshit tests to take, or just thought we were freakin' nuts. (My girlfriend was especially excited since, in her mind, there was no doubt that I was just going to hook up with some other girl.) Our recruiting efforts were unsuccessful, so we were on our own. We said our good-byes and headed off.

It was 9:00 P.M. Sunday night when we left campus. We drove through the night, taking turns every two hours. It was brutal. February in the Northeast isn't very nice, and this night was no exception. Snow for the first eight hours of the trip made for some slow going.

> One out of every three motor vehicle accidents can be attributed to driver fatigue.

As we approached Myrtle at about 9:00 A.M., the skies were clear and the weather was perfect (actually there were record temperatures for the day: 87 degrees). We needed to get to the Sea Mist.

It felt like being home. From the moment we arrived, we were both convinced that we had made the right decision. Sure, we were going to miss classes, tests, and papers, but all of those responsibilities seemed very minor compared with the pure joy of a Sea Mist breakfast.

We told our tale and got our meals comped. Then we headed for the beach. We sunned ourselves for a couple of hours and managed to meet some very nice-looking young ladies, who were all too eager to hear our tale of adventure. We hung out for a bit, but hooking up wasn't on our minds. We had a different calling, a game that wouldn't be played up in central New York for another five months: golf.

We hit the links, swung the sticks, and both broke eighty. By then it was 4:00 P.M. and almost time to head back. We had a couple of cocktails at the Shamrock Pub and then made our final faithful stop: Krispy Kreme, where we picked up a couple of dozen of those sugary gems and began our trek home.

We again drove through the night and made it back at around 5:00 A.M. I even managed to get up for my 9:00 A.M. class.

The Great Adventure was over, but the story will never fade.

—*SUNY—Cortland*

LESSON LEARNED: Don't sit around waiting for a worthy cause. A twenty-four-hour road trip doesn't need to involve the hunt for an ancient relic. Awesome waffles are a perfectly acceptable motivation. And they go better with syrup.

Midnight in Rosebud

I went to Erskine, a small college in South Carolina. Erskine was too small to have connections to your typical university fraternities. We had "literary societies," and our society president, Scott, happened to be my best friend. Scott was one of two students on campus from the state of

> Bama: Someone who is out of style and out of touch with what's going on.

Alabama, so naturally he earned the nickname "Bama." He was a big guy with dark brown hair, around six foot one, 235 pounds, and he loved to tell stories that always started out "One time, back in Alabama . . ."

Along with my friends Edelin and Otis, we made it a tradition to make a road trip to Scott's hometown during Christmas break. He lived near the booming metropolis known as Oak Hill, Alabama, in an inconsequential little suburb known as Rosebud.

So there we were: four college guys hanging out in rural Alabama, trying to figure out how to have fun in creative ways. We had already made the road trip to Montgomery and visited Hank Williams Sr.'s grave. We had already visited the town of Camden, Alabama, where Bama got his haircut. We had done just about every activity unique to the area we could think of doing. Then Bama had it: "Oh, y'all know what we should do?" he said. "We need to get Deddy's truck and go out lookin' for deer."

"You mean go out spotting deer with your headlights?" Edelin asked. "Isn't that illegal this time of year?"

Bama just grinned: "Not when you're doing it on your own property. Besides, it isn't like we're gonna shoot 'em."

It actually sounded like a lot of fun. So off we went, into the dark Alabama night, armed with just our curiosity, our southern pride, and a four-by-four. We drove a few miles down some country road and then turned down a dirt trail that led deep into the woods on "Deddy's" land. Then we came out of the woods and onto some large pastures. The trail was becoming increasingly muddy, but Bama was doing a nice job navigating the ruts formed by previous drives. Every now and then, Edelin would point out deer, whose eyes would reflect brightly from the headlights of our truck.

Everything was going great until Bama took the truck into some ruts in the trail that were way too deep. In this part of the trail there just happened to be extremely soft mud, and we were stopped dead in our tracks. In fact, we were stuck up to the truck's axles. Bama got out and trudged around in the mud looking for some sign of hope. There were some two-by-fours in the truck bed, and Edelin suggested that if we somehow jammed those far enough under one of the tires, the truck might be able to push itself out of the mud. We jammed the two-by-fours as far under the back tires as we could, and Bama got back in and revved up the engine a little. The wheels just spun mud out in all directions. The truck wasn't going anywhere. "Well, looks like we're just going to have to hike it, fellas," Bama said.

"Does anyone have a flashlight?" I asked nervously. The deafening sound of silence told me all I needed to know. There we were, in the middle of nowhere. It was dark as hell and we had no flashlight, and we had to hike back to the main road. Yee-haw! I couldn't wait! On top of that, Bama said he thought he knew the way back, but he wasn't sure. Great!

We were moving along pretty well, despite the dark, when a startled Otis suddenly stopped and said, "What the hell is this?" Apparently he had run his hand along something furry. Before anyone could respond, we heard a deep "Mooooooo!" We were surrounded by cows. Holy crap!

Bama assured us, "Don't worry, guys. There aren't any bulls in this group. We should *probably* be okay." Say what? We were careful not to startle any of the beasts, but they kept on mooing, keeping us on edge.

Just as we thought the cows were getting accustomed to our presence, we heard some howling in the distance. That's right—howling. The cows got a little restless and started shifting around uneasily. Worse yet, the howling was getting closer! Bama whispered, "I don't think we need to worry. I've heard that howling when I was with Deddy before. He said it was just coyotes. Of course, we were sitting in a tree stand with rifles at the time. . . ."

We didn't exactly want to wait around to find out, so we started double timing it. Soon we could actually see some sort of clearing ahead, and Bama said we were on the right track: "We'll be coming up on the gate soon. I definitely know the way from there." Unfortunately, the coyotes were still following us, and we could hear their howls getting closer. Finally we reached the road, panting, and grateful that we hadn't become coyote food.

A lot of people can say they've had adventures in college, talking of parties and how smashed they got. But it isn't every day that you go out spotlighting deer in the middle of the night, get stuck in the mud, go hiking through the woods without a flashlight, go cow-tipping by accident, and get chased by howling coyotes, all in one night . . . in a place called Rosebud, Alabama.

—*Erskine College*

Alumni Update: "I'm a physical education teacher in South Carolina. My friend Otis is now a church organist in Atlanta, and 'Bama' is a lawyer in Montgomery."

LESSON LEARNED: Being scared shitless is a cleansing experience. Sometimes you need that fight-or-flight response to give you perspective on life—as well as to turbocharge some intestinal evacuation.

Floored and Floored

I had just turned nineteen and decided to make the road trip to the University of Illinois to go to the bars, because in Bloomington you have to be twenty-one to get in. My fake ID wasn't good enough to use here.

So with a few buddies from home and a bunch from school, I headed out. We got to U of I around 8:30 P.M., "pre-gamed" in a friend's room, and then, at around 10:00 P.M., headed out to Kamz.

I got in with no problem since it was my b-day, and actually got a very nice "Happy birthday" from this mean-looking bouncer. We started throwing 'em back, consuming a variety of tasty elixirs including pitchers of beer, Long Islands, and Jäger bombs.

A "Jäger Bomb" consists of Jägermeister and Red Bull.

At around 1:00 A.M., we decided to head over to a bar called Tonic. At this point, things started to go downhill—really, really fast. I decided that the bathroom line was too long, so I began peeing under the table we were sitting at. Not a good idea, to say the least, but hey, no worries, right? Soon thereafter, a friend of mine from U of I called another friend to come pick us up.

I was hoping we were going home, but alas, we ended up back at this big house were I guess all the U of I gymnastics team lived. The guy who picked us up brought out a case of the never-bitter beer, and we started playing beer pong. It was me and another guy against two girls.

We were whipping their asses as I recall, though considering my level of inebriation it's difficult to say this with much certainty. What I *can* say with certainty, since it was confirmed by everyone in attendance, is that I had turned into a babbling idiot. At one point I started a fight about how our school's mascot, Reggie the Redbird, was *soooo* much cooler than U of I's stupid little Indian.

There I was, just babbling away, when I heard a thunderous crash. I thought perhaps someone had tackled me from behind because I was suddenly looking at the underside of the beer pong table. In reality, I had completely fallen through the floor in this broke-ass house. No joke. The floor had just buckled under me. Now, I'm no fatty: about twenty pounds short of the two-hundred-pound mark.

I had fallen through the floor like in the cartoons, and my feet were dangling through the ceiling of the basement. Man, was I fucking embarrassed! Everyone was laughing their asses off. One guy puked in the garbage can, he was laughing so hard. All I could say was, "Please help me."

People went into the basement and took pictures of my dangling feet, and of my half-stuck torso upstairs. By the time they pulled me out, I was so tired that I promptly passed out on their couch.

—*Illinois State University*

LESSON LEARNED: Keep your feet planted firmly on the ground, no matter where you travel—even if the ground isn't firm. Or maybe the lesson is: never underestimate the sketchy conditions that young adults will live in.

CHAPTER 19

Seven-Day Hedonists

An Anthology of Spring Breaks

Some call spring break a rite of passage. If so, it might be officially the most kick-ass rite of passage in history. Nothing beats taking a "break" from drinking, partying, and hooking up like drinking, partying, and hooking up.

Our solemn oath as the curators of college exploits demands that we defend this yearly ritual. Those seven days in March (or April, if your school is weird) represent an all-consuming goal—like the big white whale hunted by Ahab . . . but one armed with beer bongs and ankle tattoos.

The best part of spring break, though, is that it represents a duality. On one hand, it's complete and utter anarchy—tribes of feral, half-naked kids going so ape-shit that it's surprising they don't kill Piggy and take his conch, and his oversize plastic mug. (That's two high school English references, if you're counting.)

On the other hand, all of this doesn't just happen by accident. Take into consideration the logistical planning, the geometry of sleeping thirty-one girls to a room with a clogged toilet, and the economics of surviving on only Purple Hooters and Hot Pockets. Add it up and you'll see that spring break is a finals project unto itself—and not one of those easy student-athlete projects, either.

So get out your red pens and see how you'd grade these efforts.

Hanging with the Girls

I couldn't understand why my girlfriend, or her friends, wanted me there, but I was an absolute *hero* for going on spring break with the gals, rather than with my guy friends. (In reality, I just couldn't afford to go where the guys had gone, but what the chicks didn't know, didn't hurt 'em.)

Back on campus, these ladies shared a two-bedroom quad and were pretty chummy. My almost daily presence there led to this herd getting real used to me, and they just considered me "one of the gals." They'd talk about the guys they were dating, the guys they *wanted* to be dating, the gross ones, the great ones, etc. They'd talk about kittens, Boone's Farm, fuzzy slippers, jogging in the quad, how fat their asses were, and

Boone's Farm "wine" is produced by E&J Gallo Winery. It is not technically a wine, but rather a hyperemasculated malt beverage.

whose turn it was to leave the societal-changing deep comment on their dorm door dry-erase board for all the world to see. I didn't mind it, it was all so entertaining.

Rather than dispense with the usual details of what spring break was like (you've seen it on TV), I'd like to share a smaller tale, a tale of woe, of em-

Tom Bodet, the voice of Motel 6, also lends his voice to Steven Spielberg's *Animaniacs* series.

barrassment, and of a spring break mishap. Sure, there were about one hundred underage college students running amok at this thirty-nine-

dollar-per-night Motel 6, but that wasn't the interesting part. You've seen *Revenge of the Nerds*. It's been done.

The interesting part, to me, was that these four girls were attempting to share a bathroom all week, something they didn't have to do back at the dorms. I was continually mesmerized by all the beauty and skin care products, the towels and bathing suits, and the general filth that overwhelmed that room. My lone toothbrush and bar of soap cowered in a corner, too scared to come out and join the fun. It looked as though the health and beauty aisles at Rite Aid had collided with the cheesy tourist traps that hawk eye-blinding towels and stringy neon bikinis. Four freshman girls doing whatever it takes to put their best faces and bodies forward—and two male eyes to take it all in.

As I sat on the porch one evening, talking to whoever passed by, the gals were inside getting ready. It looked like a commercial for tampons, the way they all tried to get at the mirror at once, with scanty club clothing on, laughing all the while. My girlfriend had been pleading with me all week to try to find a guy to hook up with her "not-so-fair" friend, Kendra. Kendra didn't have the greatest luck back home, but she was a nice girl, so I did what I could. From the friendly drunken crew outside, I wrangled up a couple of guys who seemed pretty cool and were looking to have a good time that evening. Unbeknownst to me, the ladies were inside chatting away about "that time of the month"—the reason Kendra would be able to get only "so lucky" that evening.

My girlfriend was saying how she craved Boston cream pies once every twenty-eight days. Another said she could eat a chocolate bar the size of an $8\frac{1}{2}$ 3 11 sheet of paper, and Kendra chimed in with her feat of having eaten half a box of chocolate doughnuts earlier that day. Giggle, giggle. Just then I brought the guys into the room, and pleasantries were exchanged. One guy asked to use the bathroom. The toilet flushed, and he came out as introductions were ending. Following his exit, a trickle of water flowed from an overflowing toilet.

Suntan lotion bottles were like log flumes on the slow and steady stream of chocolaty water. Used makeup pads bobbed like water lilies. All those expensive towels and bathing suits were now permanently tainted. At least my toothbrush and soap were safe!

I felt really bad for this guy, until I saw that Kendra's face was raw-steak red. While the guy was desperately pleading his innocence to a stunned and silent room, Kendra ran out of the room and toward the beach.

Apparently she hadn't wanted to throw the rest of her doughnuts in the trash can, for fear that she would eat the rest of them. (Yes, even *after* they had been in the trash can.) So she had decided to flush them down the toilet. She had clogged the crapper with half a box of mini chocolate doughnuts. Did nobody take a dump all day?

Everyone on our floor who passed by our room would tell a friend to come look. Some even found out why maintenance was there (gee, who could have spread such info?), and before long, the entire hotel knew. The guy I originally had in mind for Kendra saw me doubled over on the balcony, and asked if it were true. I couldn't lie. I mean, Kendra gave herself away by running out of the room. Too damn funny. One of his buddies yelled, "Hey, man, then she's *perfect* for you!"

We left Florida a day early. Kendra laughs about it now.

—*University of Maryland*

LESSON LEARNED: Secrets in life are hard to hide. No matter how hard you try to suppress them and obfuscate the truth, they will always come floating back up. Metaphorically speaking, of course.

Moms Gone Wild

A bunch of my frat brothers and I went to Mardi Gras for spring break, and it was a hell of a time—except, that is, for one horrid event that is burned into both my mind and that of my friend Danny.

Danny and I were walking around with beads around our neck, beers in our hands, and with tits all around us. Life was good! We had split from

> It's considered inappropriate and disrespectful to wear Mardi Gras beads during Lent.

the rest of our crew a little earlier and were talking to some ladies and having a blast, when it happened. We saw a group of older women (think: early forties). But they still looked good!

I noticed one of the women looked familiar, but I couldn't place her. Anyway, they wanted a picture of some hunky guys (us) to show their husbands that they were still young (and desirable?). Danny and I agreed to pose with them. Then the women flashed us, I guess to show their thanks.

Danny and I didn't think much about this as we enjoyed our remaining three days. On our way back to school, a few of us decided to pay a visit to our buddy Craig. He was at his family's house in southern Mississippi, and the visit afforded us a golden opportunity to stretch out and score some free grub!

As we stood in the kitchen, Craig's mom came walking down the stairs. Danny and I took one look at her and immediately turned around to catch our breath. One of the women who had flashed us earlier that week on Bourbon Street was none other than Craig's mom!

> Tadpoling refers to a relationship between a younger man and an older woman.

When she saw us in the kitchen, she turned bright red. Craig said, "Mom, you remember Danny and Brian [me]." She couldn't even look at us. Craig then proceeded to ask, "Mom, how was visiting Aunt Laura and Aunt Michelle?" It was all Danny and I could do not to burst out laughing. It's been a couple of years, and Danny and I have never told Craig or, for that matter, anyone else. I'm guessing the pictures were burned.

—*University of Mississippi*

LESSON LEARNED: You never know who's out there. Remember this the next time you decide to urinate, undress, or bump and grind in public. And don't forget: that boob you paid good beads to see may be attached to someone's relative.

Toppled and Topless

Let me preface this story by saying that I don't know how to swim. It's baffling, but my dad wouldn't let us take swimming lessons at the public pool because kids peed in it. This is also the reason for my obsessive-compulsive disorder, which is a totally different story. I used to say that I could swim to save my life, but as you will soon learn, I can no longer make that claim.

Spring break in Acapulco my senior year promised to be a week of sunbathing on the beach by day and dancing on the bars by night. A few hundred of our closest friends from Villanova descended upon this famed Mexican resort.

Monday afternoon the weather was perfect, if not a little hot, and everyone was enjoying a rousing game of "Who would you bang first?" when my friend Kevin started complaining that no one would go in the water with him. "It's so hot. Doesn't anyone want to swim? Whine, whine . . ." Sick of his whining, I volunteered to go for a dip. Unlike the Long Island beaches to which I am accustomed, the ocean there was completely empty, a telling sign of a strong undertow—a point completely lost on me.

> Acapulco's Condesa Beach is fairly rough and is considered dangerous for swimming most of the year because of the undertow.

Prancing down to the water's edge in my J.Crew bathing suit that tied on the sides and my most beloved Burberry sunglasses, I repeatedly told

Kevin that I was only going to wade in to my knees. After only minutes in the cool water, a giant wave quickly swept me out a good forty feet from where I had been wading. I couldn't get my head above the water, I couldn't touch the ocean floor, and I started to panic. In the next minute, another giant wave sucked me under the water and dragged my body to the shore. While in the current, I actually believed I was going to die. "I am going to be the girl who dies on spring break," I thought. "How embarrassing for my parents!" Well, the wave receded, and I clumsily stood up facing out into the ocean. I needed a moment to compose myself and fish my contacts out of the back of my brain.

Grateful to be alive and breathing, I heard my friend Eric calling behind me. "Amy, don't move. I'm going to get you a towel," he said. What? Why do I need a towel? I looked down, and I was completely naked! The top of my bathing suit was around my waist, and the bottom was floating somewhere in Acapulco Bay. Suddenly, I was very aware of my surroundings, and I instinctively got on my knees to shield my naked body (a reflex for which I would later take a lot of heat). As Eric ran up the beach screaming, "She lost her bathing suit," the Villanova classes of 2003 and 2004 began staring, pointing, and taking pictures. However, the force of the current was again too strong, and as I was being tossed around, my kneecap dislocated. Once again I was drowning, only now, in about two feet of water. To complete this three-ring spectacle, the Mexican lifeguard arrived with his big orange buoy to save my naked self.

What happens on spring break stays at spring break. Unless you share the tale on our site. Visit CollegeStories.com/springbreak to read more.

Finally, my friend Petra (apparently the only one not doubled over laughing) came down with a towel. While hobbling out of the water because my knee was in so much pain,

I have learned an enormous amount from this experience, namely that no one actually *dies* of embarrassment . . . because if someone were going to, it would have been me! I also learned that laughing at yourself is a very good way to cope with any situation. Now, let's be serious—the greatest lesson is that I need to learn to swim!

—author Amy Pellicane

I must have gone into shock, as apparently I started yelling to the Mexican lifeguard (who had just saved my life) to go back into the water and

172 ■ CLASS DISMISSED

find my Burberry sunglasses. Then two Australian strangers offered me a piggyback ride. There was no escaping the humiliation when I finally got back to my lounge chair.

Determined not to let this ruin the rest of my trip (or my life), I iced my knee, popped a few ibuprofen, and laughed with the rest of my friends about how I, of all people, got naked on the beach on spring break!

Later that night, in classic spring break form at Señor Frog's, all of the boys offered me their Mardi Gras beads, assuring me that I had definitely earned them. Slightly limping, somewhat embarrassed, and severely intoxicated was how I spent the rest of the night—if only I knew with confidence that no photographic evidence existed, I could truly look back with no regrets.

—*Villanova University*

Alumni Update: Since graduation, the author has been working in the Public Relations Department of Lancôme in New York.

LESSON LEARNED: Nature is a sublimely awesome force. Some people realize this when they hike along a mountain ridge or ponder the vastness of the plains. Others do so when they get molested by an ocean wave.

CHAPTER 20

International Procrastination

A Study in Studying Abroad

Nothing quite inspires students to think outside the cinder-block dorm room like a trip across the globe.

If you want academic reasons to study abroad, then just pick up the glossy brochures from the school. But anyone who's done it can tell you that "studying abroad" is pronounced with a silent "studying." Some call it experiencing the culture; others call it sampling the international party scene, urinating on historic landmarks, and destroying innocent dinnerware (if you studied in Greece).

The biggest lesson learned from all of these travels is certainly not in those pass/fail classes. The real value is that studying abroad is the ultimate test of one's resourcefulness—like a semester-long episode of *Survivor.* You need to make do with only a sockful of money, a remedial understanding of the native language, and all of your belongings wadded up in the bottom of an Arctic-expedition backpack. And most students still can outwit and outplay their way around foreign lands.

But regardless of your actual experience, the real payoff from these travels is when you get back to campus and share your stories. Not to mention your new distaste for American beer and your voracious smoking habit.

We've selected three of our favorite tales for your stateside reading pleasure, so grab your passport and come along.

Greek Toga

We were a total of thirty-two females from the University of Florida, on a summer trip traveling through Greece. We were even receiving credit toward our majors on this island-hopping adventure. Our first free weekend rolled around, and instead of doing something culturally significant, twenty-one of us did something even better. We made a pilgrimage to what was rumored to be the Mecca of wild and crazy times, the Everest of European party destinations: the Pink Palace in Corfu.

> The Pink Palace purports to be "Corfu's World Famous Travellers & Backpackers' Haven Resort for 20 years and counting."

Getting there proved to be half the battle. Being on a college budget, some of us tried to save a little money by taking the bus from the outskirts of Athens. It was like leaving the crux of world civilization and then seeing where it went wrong, all in one cab ride. We're talking thirteen hours of bus transfers, ferry hopping, random stopping, and death-defying driving on curvaceous mountain roads. This experience was shared with forty of the creepiest men imaginable, who smelled like freshly soured milk and stared at you while you slept. After what seemed like an eternity, we finally arrived in Corfu at 6:00 A.M. A man named Pinocchio greeted us and showed us to our pink travel bus.

Old Pinocchio told us we had to make a quick stop at the airport to pick up a group of thirteen girls who would be arriving within the hour. Of course, it was none other than the remaining thirteen girls from our program, who had decided to shell out the extra fifty euros and were able to get some much needed shut-eye, and oh yeah, bypass the living, breathing glimpse into Hell that was our bus ride.

Pinocchio decided that all of us weary travelers needed some music, and what would be more appropriate before the hour of 7:00 A.M. than everyone's favorite techno tune, "I Want to Be Your Underwear (So I Can Feel You Everywhere)." We laughed in amazement at our situation, and Pinocchio also laughed, staring directly down my well-endowed friend's shirt as he drove the mountain roads.

At the Pink Palace, we were given a speech by a young man who was trying to earn money for the next leg of his travels, and getting ass each night from drunken travelers. Our boy Collin explained the rules: drink our alcohol all day and night, go to dinner and stay for happy hour from 8:00 to 10:00 P.M. or visit the twenty-four-hour bar, and return the toga material the next day or you'll have to pay for it. Simple enough. Then, when the hour reached 7:30 A.M., we were all given a welcome shot of ouzo. Cheers, *yammas,* and *opa*!

The toga party took place on Saturday night. Everyone, male and female alike, had to wear a pink toga starting at dinner, or you couldn't eat. This all took place in the Palladium, a bunker-like dining hall with a massive dance floor. After traversing the five hundred extremely steep steps, you were seated with people you didn't know, so as to further encourage the drunk mingling. Also, the drinks were super cheap, so no one felt bad about ordering one, five, or thirteen more than they normally would. Happy hour immediately followed dinner.

Following happy hour was the main event, where all of the drunken backpackers working at the Pink Palace tried to emulate traditional Greek dancing and other Greek "traditions." Good intentions, but the execution had room for improvement. They started by asking us to form a huge circle on the dance floor, about 150 strong.

Our boy Collin and some other guy started walking around the circle, first giving you a shot of ouzo, or three in my case, and following it up, not with a chaser but with a plate smashed over your head. It truly didn't occur to us, until much later, that all 150 of us shared the same shot glass. After the entire circle was both pleasantly numbed and experiencing a headache, two lucky people, both from our program, were taken to the center to get an entire stack of plates smashed over their heads, with shots of ouzo before and after each plate.

> Plate breaking is part of the Greek concept of *kefi,* "spontaneous good humor and fun."

It was an epic night, but all good things must come to an end, and eventually back to Athens we had to go. Don't think for a second that we didn't join our friends this time on Olympic Airlines. But damn it if I wasn't still a few sheets to the wind in the airport, lost my boarding pass as a result, and was finally told I had to purchase yet another plane ticket to get back.

This party definitely would have made the boys of *Animal House* proud. Toga! Toga! Toga! The lesson? In Europe, don't take the cheap way out. Save that for the States, where you speak the language.

—*University of Florida*

LESSON LEARNED: Since she did the lesson for us, we're taking a break on this one. Please feel free to take a break yourself, preferably to smash some plates and light shit on fire.

Giovanni's Ego

Cortona is not a place you forget. The view is locked in my mind—I can still see the worn cobblestone and the stuccoed houses that line the streets.

I went there the fall of my senior year on a study abroad art program. I had always wanted to go to Italy, and Cortona offered itself to me—an Italian village nestled on the side of a mountain.

Cortona is a small town in Tuscany, Italy, famous as the base for some scenes in Roberto Benigni's film *Life Is Beautiful.*

There were about fifty of us—American students from all over the country brought together to do what twenty-year-olds do in Europe: walk, visit museums, philosophize about the world, eat incredible food, and drink a hell of a lot of *vino.*

So that was what we did. And we had our favorite bar, a hole-in-the-wall where we'd hang out with the locals, most of whom spoke English nearly as well as we did. I loved it there because they had this big TV that all the Italian guys congregated around to watch soccer, a topic I knew much about. I had played it since I was a little girl, up until my junior year in college, when I had to give it up because I'd had three surgeries on my left knee.

I missed the sport terribly, so it was great to sit at those tables with a drink, watching the games. It was all boys—a few Americans and a handful of Italians—plus me.

One of the Italians, an excruciatingly obnoxious boy named Giovanni, was always bragging about how good he was, about all the amazing things he could do with the ball. He went on and on and on, eventually challenging the American boys to a game.

Boys being boys, they immediately agreed, and the two sides began to taunt each other incessantly. But Giovanni was definitely the worst of the bunch, ranting about his god-given "futbol" talent. I remember him pointing up to the moving figures on the screen and saying, "I'm even good enough to be on TV!"

Unable to hold back any longer, I asked him, "So why aren't you, then?" The room got quiet.

Giovanni looked over at me, and I winked at him. He smirked and asked if I wanted to play. He even went as far as to say that if I was actually any good, he'd buy me a drink. I agreed, which surprised him because Italians aren't used to girls playing over there. I probably shouldn't have agreed to play, given the state of my knee, but caution isn't always one of my strengths.

> The United States women's national soccer team has won two of the four Women's World Cups and two of the three Olympic women's tournaments held to date.

So two days later, a ragtag group of us met the Italians out on this small turf field in the center of town. Night game, under the lights, in the middle of a soccer field in Tuscany . . . it just doesn't get much better than that.

Giovanni was in rare form that night, talking nonstop smack. On the very first play of the game, he got the ball and dribbled it down the field, right in front of the goal. Just as he was about to shoot it, I came in from the other side and tackled the ball away so that he came down hard on his hip and rolled a couple of feet. A few of the other guys chuckled. Giovanni got up, flustered, and brushed himself off as he cursed rapidly in Italian. We finished the game tied one to one, and Giovanni pouted the whole time.

The following week we all went up to the bar again. When I got there, I noticed a glass of red wine unaccompanied at the far end of the table. Giovanni motioned me over and pointed to the glass. I sat down in front of it and looked over at him. He raised his Guinness up high in the air, took a big swig, and gave me a little nod.

Best damn night I spent in Cortona.

—*Furman University*

Alumni Update: The author is currently enrolled in Columbia University's Master of Fine Arts program in Creative Writing.

LESSON LEARNED: There are few joys in life to match that of shutting up an obnoxious braggart—especially if the end result involves sitting in a bar in Italy sipping red wine.

The Swedish Attaché

"Oh, you dog. You're in love with her!" exclaimed Berlie, my senior-year roommate. It was 1955, the college was Washington and Lee University in Lexington, Virginia. "It's too bad she can't come for Fancy Dress," Berlie said. "I mean it is *the* collegiate dance in the South."

"She doesn't know that," I said. "She's from Sweden. I'm sure they've never heard of Fancy Dress there! It's just too bad she has a friend coming over from Sweden. But I understand." If her friend wanted to be an exchange student like Elisabeth, I'd do everything I could to help her.

Elisabeth Stenbeck from Stockholm. Relatively tall, slender, and yes, blond. For one who had only studied English from books, her spoken English was outstanding. But her French was even better after a year at the Sorbonne. I still think I detected a scent of Norway spruce about her.

> The 1912 Olympics held in Stockholm, Sweden, starred Jim Thorpe, who won both the pentathlon and the decathlon.

The theme for Fancy Dress that year was Elizabethan England. I swear Elisabeth could have replaced my history professor in discussing the times and the dress. She was a handsome, regal woman.

Elisabeth could not come to Fancy Dress because of her visiting friend, and that was that. So I got a date from Sweet Briar, or was it Randolph-Macon Women's College?

Later that year I took Elisabeth to our Fiji Island Party at the Phi Gam House. Berlie and the fraternity brothers had decorated the basement with foliage from the tennis nets to give the place an island feel. Someone unknowingly gathered poison ivy among the foliage and Berlie's eyes, face, and parts of his body swelled up. Serious stuff, but Elisabeth chuckled when she heard of Berlie's misfortune. It must have been Swedish schadenfreude.

As graduation approached, I wondered what would become of our relationship. I thought of myself as being "smitten" with Elisabeth. Yes, that's what it was—smitten! She and I did correspond for a brief period afterward—through the summer and into the fall, when I went into the army. But shortly afterward it stopped.

The break was complete.

Bonn, West Germany, 1964

"Pat, do you want to go to this reception?" I asked my wife. "We received an invitation today from the Swiss ambassador. As you know, we're not required to go, but it might be fun."

When we arrived at the Swiss ambassador's residence, cars were searching for parking places and a small line had formed outside the main entrance. I turned to the man standing by us and jokingly said in German, "That serves us right for being on time. Now wait. We have an old military saying, 'Hurry up and wait.' "

"Yes, we have something similar in our army," he joked back. He introduced himself: he was the Swedish economic attaché.

Shoptalk ensued: the German monetary and fiscal policies, the cost of maintaining troops in Europe . . . then the wife of the Swedish attaché came bouncing into the conversation.

After introductions, I said to her, "I hate to play the 'Whom do you know?' game, but I only know one person in Sweden. She's from Stockholm. . . ."

"I'm from Goteburg, but my husband is from Stockholm and he knows everyone there," she replied.

I turned back to the ambassador just as my wife came up. "I really know only one person in Sweden, in Stockholm actually. Your wife says you're from Stockholm and know everybody there. Do you happen to know an Elisabeth Stenbeck?" I asked.

There was a noticeable pause. A quizzical look came over his face and he squinted.

"Yes . . . yes, I know her well. I was engaged to her when she was studying in the States, in Virginia. I visited her at college. We broke up not long after she returned from the States. She's married now. Last time I heard about her, she had a child on the way. We haven't kept in touch."

Could he have been the "friend" who visited Elisabeth during Fancy Dress, a person I had assumed was female? My long inhale must have been noticeable—or was it the expression on my face?

His wife, turning to mine, said, "I think we should let the boys talk about their old girlfriend."

Both women had impish smiles as they turned away.

Nine years and 3,500 miles . . . and I just now learn of my rival for Elisabeth's heart.

—*Washington and Lee University*

Alumni Update: After graduating from Washington and Lee, Arthur Fern was a counterintelligence agent in 1950s Berlin. Following a master's at SAIS, Johns Hopkins, he was in international finance at the U.S. Treasury, was an attaché at the U.S. embassy (Bonn), and was in consulting in Congress. Later, he established a firm in D.C. to work on World Bank projects, traveling in some forty countries. His upcoming book, *The Joy of Odyssey,* encourages young adults and career changers to enter international work.

LESSON LEARNED: Women, like the writings of James Joyce or the cafeteria in your school's food court, harbor secrets you'll never fully comprehend—a double entendre here, a meatloaf surprise or a secret attaché lover there.

THE AMAZING COLLEGE STUDENT

Genius, when young, is divine.

—Benjamin Disraeli, British Prime Minister

We've learned a lot about this creature that is the North American college student. It mates a lot, but not particularly well. It's highly adaptable, especially to the squalor of its own filth. It lives a largely nocturnal existence but still finds time to sleep in class.

But what reading these college tales offers is a glimpse into many forms of genius. And one of those forms happens to be a nineteen-year-old technically homeless intellectual-in-training.

All kidding aside, the college student is quite an amazing creature. Given the right motivation, its creative problem-solving skills are unparalleled. Its sense of humor can be impressively cunning and adroit. Its air of indestructibility is completely unwarranted. And it must have something special, since it seems to be so damn lucky it can make you sick.

For some of you who have read the previous chapters, an appreciation for the college student has not rubbed off on you yet. In this final section, prepare to be rubbed off on. Here you will find a handful of the top stories submitted to the site.

Now that we've sufficiently overhyped this final installment, please take a minute, lower your expectations, and enjoy these final chapters. They'll certainly give you new reason to have faith in America's youth. Kind of.

CHAPTER 21

Busting Balls and Exploding Ovens

In Defense of Classic Pranking and Revenge

Revengeful pranks are a society's way of self-regulation. Like Adam Smith's invisible hand or torching reviews on eBay, these activities are a community's Warren G and Nate Dogg: the regulators. They keep egos sufficiently deflated and 'tudes appropriately in check. They make sure that privileges are earned and constant paranoia is fostered. And best of all, pranks beget pranks, creating a perpetual-motion machine of stupid behavior. And who wouldn't love that?

You might be asking yourself, isn't this all just immature time-wasting from people who should know better? And you would be right. But pranks give us lessons in employing divergent thinking skills and practicing improvisational problem solving to achieve a higher goal. What is that goal? Often it involves bringing a buddy back to earth by seriously busting his balls.

So here is our salute to the classic college prank: may your sheets be shorted and your shorts stolen, but never sheet your shorts.

Lou Can't Be Beet

I was a sophomore at Assumption in those days, and Lou, well, Lou simply transcended any particular year. He was more like a "presence" on campus at that point—much talked about, but seen only in fleeting glimpses. You see, Lou's wild ways were about to catch up with him, and he knew it. He knew his tenuous grasp on a diploma was close to slipping away, but he also knew he couldn't deny his basic nature, which was, of course, Mr. Hyde to the average person's Jekyll.

And that's how we came to be at that Clark University party that night. It was a Friday and Louie was looking for some action. He'd heard that a bunch of Clarkies were having a bit of a "par-doo," so we drove over to investigate. We paid the three-dollar

Clark is the oldest graduate institution in the United States.

cover for the keg and went inside. We were rather underwhelmed. The music sucked. The beer was a pony keg, and they were having a hard time killing off *that*. But believe it or not, Lou—the twenty-five-year-old professional drunk—was being rather affable. Unfortunately, the Clarkies were not. They were a rather snobby lot, and often answered Lou's friendly conversational gambits by turning on their heels and walking away.

After about thirty minutes, Lou had had enough. As he walked through the kitchen, I saw him quickly reach out and turn the oven on to five hundred degrees. I caught up with him in the hallway and asked him why he'd done that. He simply motioned me outside and went over to the trunk of his car. And there, inside the trunk, was a number ten can of beets. Yes, children, you heard me. A number 10 can of beets—the industrial-size can ordered by restaurants and

Beets have the highest sugar content of any vegetable.

state hospitals. Lou had acquired this can of beets somewhere during his travels and had hung on to it, waiting for "the right occasion."

And that occasion was now. Lou put the can under his coat and went back inside. When I caused a momentary distraction in the kitchen, he opened the oven door and placed the can of beets inside. "Now what do we do?" I asked him.

He raised his beer to his lips, took a sip, and smiled slightly. "Now we wait." We walked into the living room, where we found some actual friendly people with whom we engaged in conversation. And it was an interesting conversation, too. Politics, I think. In fact, I became so engrossed that I wondered for a second what could be the cause of the loud *THOMP* that rang through the house about ten minutes later. But the screams that followed snapped me back to the matter at hand.

Everyone rushed into the kitchen. About twenty traumatized people were covered in purple beet juice and picking beet shrapnel out of their hair. Lou turned and casually clapped me on the shoulder.

"Now we leave," he said softly. He stole the pony keg on his way out.

—*Assumption College*

LESSON LEARNED: Random subversion can keep the social strata nicely cracked. You need people like Lou to keep people like the Clarkies in their place with acts like a beet bomb.

Toasted in Bed

During my sophomore year at the University of Montana, I lived with my brother and best friend in an off-campus apartment. We developed a habit of messing with one another when any of us were drunk. It was usually pretty harmless stuff, such as writing on the passed-out person's face or putting their bed on the lawn. Normally nobody else was affected by our hijinks.

One winter night, I was at a keg party in the woods and was working hard to score with this girl, a hottie on the volleyball team. We spent the night talking, drinking, flirting, and eventually making out.

When it was time to head back to town, she asked if I'd give her a ride home. I said "Sure," thinking that I was sure to get lucky.

When we got back to my place, she wasted no time in getting naked and was soon sitting on my bed waiting for me. Blessing my good fortune, I quickly undressed in front of her and then turned off the lights. We made out for a while on top of the sheets, and then climbed under the sheets. . . .

Shortly after getting under the sheets, she yelled out, "What the fuck is this?"

Confused, I turned on the lights. My brother and best friend had filled my bed with peanut butter toast! Not just a slice or two, but several loaves. From the foot of the bed to the headboard, my queen-size bed was covered in peanut butter toast!

I couldn't help but laugh my ass off. While I was laughing and losing any thought of having sex with this girl, she passed out cold and fell face first right into the toast.

> The toaster was invented in 1491 by an obscure French alchemist by the name of Gérard Depardieu (no relation to the actor).

I did the gentlemanly thing and covered her up, and I slept on the couch.

Despite my efforts, the next morning she woke up completely pissed off. She didn't bother to shower or call a friend; she just got dressed and walked home. She must have thought that I'd done this to her. She left so quickly I didn't have a chance to explain.

> Peanut butter was widely introduced in 1904 by C. H. Sumner at the Louisiana Purchase Exposition (St. Louis World's Fair), which also popularized the ice cream cone, the hot dog, and the hamburger.

I saw her around campus over the next three years, and she simply ignored me. I had, of course, told everyone I knew about the funny story. From that night on (to many people on campus) my hot volleyball girl was known simply as "Peanut Butter."

God, I miss college!

—*University of Montana*

LESSON LEARNED: Don't discredit the power of complete and utter randomness. There is something magical about doing something to induce head scratching and confusion. Like reading seventy-plus college stories in one sitting.

Aussie STD Scare Scam

At Purdue, we have a blood drive every year. We compete against Indiana University to see who donates the most blood. Wanting to beat IU, I tried to get some people to donate blood. I ended up recruiting only one person: my Australian friend Dave, who lives above us in our apartment building.

The day came, and we went to donate blood. One of the questions on the form was "Do you have any sexually transmitted diseases?" Well, Dave had recently begun dating a girl across the street. I told him this would be a golden opportunity to test for a disease.

Later, back at the apartment, my roommate came up with the prank of a lifetime: he suggested we forge a letter to Dave, explaining that the test results indicated that he had herpes simplex 2.

We spent days on this letter—we even obtained the American Red Cross letterhead and put the Red Cross CEO's name on the letter. We included facts about herpes and what Dave should do, most important: "contact all sexual partners within the past six months."

> Herpes simplex affects primarily the mouth and genital area. Type 1 is the most common herpes simplex virus and is usually acquired in childhood. Type 2 is sexually transmitted.

This was a nice touch because Dave knew that he hadn't had herpes before coming to America, which was just that semester. So he would deduce that he had gotten it from his new lady friend. Dave's fellow Aussie roommate allowed us to use their mail key to put our fake letter into their mailbox. The letter had the American Red Cross address, Dave's address, and an American thirty-seven-cent stamp in the corner.

When Dave discovered the letter, we all went outside, trying our best to contain our laughter. He was left alone to read it. He remained noticeably sullen for the next couple of days. He drank a lot as well. We kept our silence, letting him cry inside, waiting for him to crack.

It never happened.

He didn't ever confront his new lady friend. But, we knew he was hurting inside. About five days went by, and Dave was still silent most of the time, so we knew our letter was working. But since he was our friend, we took pity on him and decided it was time to end this prank.

So we wrote another letter, saying, "We have analyzed your blood sample, as we do with all infected samples, and found that you *do not* have herpes. But, we have found that you have a far more serious disease: Abo-australian-shititus." We then signed the letter with our names.

Another couple of days went by, and Dave finally checked his mail. He took the letter to his room while the rest of us waited outside. About ten seconds later, we heard a huge laugh, and he came running outside. "You dirty cunts!" Dave kept repeating over and over.

—*Purdue University*

LESSON LEARNED: The devil is in the details. If it weren't for your amoral pranking and callous disregard for sensitivity, an employer would love your eye for detail and follow-through. Well done.

Squeal Like a Pig

The last days of the school year draw upon a part of the brain that no other times seem to affect. Faced with finals, we absorb caffeine like a Friday night beer and adopt strange behavior otherwise foreign to our natures. Such behavior was on full display on the last day of my junior year at Clemson University.

I took Anatomy that semester, which included an intense lab involving a pig. I remember the pig being part of my "textbook" expenses that year, which seemed peculiar to me. What else counted as "textbooks"? I imagined all sorts of eerie items like bull semen for Animal Husbandry and virus packets for Microbiology. But for me that semester, my text was a pickled baby pig.

For fourteen weeks, I took that pig apart muscle by blood vessel by ligament, until no millimeter was left undisturbed. By the last week, I owned a carcass held together by a spine and a skull and assorted flaps of skin and sinew, and with an odor that had ripened over the months—much like a trash can full of vodka, grain, grapes, and oranges fermented and left over from a long weekend.

> The most useful dissection tool is a blunt probe. It will easily separate tissues along natural cleavage lines, without damaging the structures being studied.

So I left my last day of lab, pig in hand, and headed to the dining hall for dinner. Meeting my boyfriend there, we talked about the countdown to leaving campus and how we'd managed to put another semester behind us. We were tired enough to be punchy, and impish enough to be dangerous. What could we do that was safe but worth telling our children about in later years?

Both of us turned to the piggy box. "Piggy needs a decent burial, don't you think?" I asked.

"Ah, yes, my dear. Methinks we should see piggy into the next world with a respectable send-off," he said, stiffening and donning a faux pipe in the form of a pencil.

"And did you have something in mind, dear sir?"

"Let's see . . . have you completed your evening meal? And was it enjoyable?" he scoffed.

I played along: "Why yes, I have, and thanks for asking. It was quite enjoyable."

"Let me take your tray, madam."

Having read his mind, I had already opened the box and untied the bag. My boyfriend gently picked up the little swine and laid it upon my plate, centering it to prevent its rolling off. I tucked leftover pieces of potato and carrots around its neck to highlight the permanent smile on its little dead face—a smile that now exposed teeth, jaw muscles, and a touch of bone here and there.

And before anyone could tell what we were doing, we picked up our books and walked the tray to the conveyor belt that carried dirty trays and dishes to the workers in the kitchen. My boyfriend saluted, and I placed my hand over my heart in reverent acknowledgment of the ultimate sacrifice the pig had made for my education. Upon saying good-bye and "Godspeed," we turned tail and quickly walked toward the door, past snickering eyes and smirks.

Placing my hand upon the door, I halted.

"AAAAAHHHHHHHH" rang from the kitchen.

"EEEEEEEEEEEEEEEEKKKKKKKK" was echoed a split second later.

Various squeals and shrieks bellowed from the end of the conveyor belt as the buxom middle-aged kitchen help in gloves and hairnets faced the fact that a cadaver had greeted them during the dinner shift.

"Such a pity," said my boyfriend.

"Yes, they must have loved him so," I said.

And with that we split, laughing our butts off in memory of the piglet and the end of our junior year.

—Clemson University

Alumni Update: "The boyfriend became my husband, then my ex-husband. As for this story, I learned how to start and enjoy innocent fun. Listening to the squeals was hilarious, and I got to feel a bit impish and let my hair down in playing the prank. This was probably one of the few times I remember having fun with my ex, and it's ironic and fateful that it involved something dead."

LESSON LEARNED: It's important to know that even the tamest, most straitlaced college student can appreciate rotting-corpse humor. When life becomes mundane, simply pull something out of your ass that'll bring a smile to your face—like a dead pig or a scream from a hardworking, innocent, middle-aged woman.

CHAPTER 22

Premeditated Mayhem

Devious Applications of Genius

The serious college student might embrace the campus experience, grabbing life by the horns. But the exceptional college student grabs life by the horns, duct-tapes it to the flagpole, and leaves life pantsed and embarrassed in front of the Kappa Delta house. "How you like me now, life?" Those are our favorite kids, the evil geniuses in the making.

In the following stories, you'll see examples of smart kids applying their knowledge to undertakings that clearly don't require a number-two pencil. Unless, of course, that pencil is being shoved up . . . well, you get the picture.

Sure, these stories represent the next level of mischief—requiring more planning, more follow-through, and way more cojones. But most important, they represent the creativity and thinking skills taught in school—which are used for projects such as screwing with friends and rival schools.

These stories support one of the most important lessons in life: a college education is never wasted, just misapplied in amazing ways—then published in a book for everyone to laugh at.

Harvard Proves It Sucks

Months of planning, hundreds of dollars, and a several-hundred-mile road trip "to scout out the stadium" had already been invested into a prank that would put Harvard to shame. My friend Mike Kai had gathered a group of around twenty loyal Elis to dress in custom-made shirts that read HARVARD PEP SQUAD. In the meantime, I, David Aulicino, had worked hard with the logistics and spent hours telling friends how to properly sort 1,800 sheets of red and white construction paper.

It looked like everything was in place for the 2004 Harvard-Yale football game. I led two or three people into the Harvard stadium with the sheets of construction paper, and we carried it into the stands. Mike Kai and the "Harvard Pep Squad" met us in the stands, and I told everyone to pair off. According to my plan, one person in each pair would simply carry the 150 to 250 sheets of paper, and the other person would pull off the top stack of paper, hand it to the first person in each row, and say, "Take the top sheet and pass the rest on." All of us

> The first football game between Harvard and Yale took place when Ulysses S. Grant was president of the United States.

transformed into Harvard students by putting on the pep squad shirts and painting red *H*s on our faces. Then we got together and realized it was time to go into action. Mike led a small group of people to the appropriate sections, where they cheered with megaphones and threw pep squad T-shirts into the crowd to try to excite the hundreds of Harvard fans.

I led the rest of the pep squad into the stands. As the first stack of construction paper was handed out, one fan asked, "We have a pep squad?" I immediately stumbled, as this was the last question I'd expected. But within a second, I responded: "We're a group of students who got to-

> A similar prank was pulled off in 1962 by the fiendish students from Cal Tech, who infiltrated the Washington Huskies pep squad.

gether so that this paper could be passed out. When everyone raises their sheet of paper, the other side will see everyone spelling out GO HARVARD in big red letters." The fan responded, half-jokingly, "You guys aren't from MIT, are you? What house are you in?" I laughed off the MIT part and replied, "I'm in Lowell." He bought it, and the paper started flying down the rows.

A stadium of Harvard fans prove their point.

Once we heard from everyone that the paper had been passed out, we ran to the front of the crowd and shouted with megaphones and held up signs saying, "Hold up your paper." Slowly a wave of paper rose across the sections until everyone was holding up their paper. Unsure if our planning had been for nothing, we suddenly heard a cheer all the way across the stadium from the Yale side. "You suck. You suck. You suck." It was in unison, and it could clearly be heard. At that point we knew we had done it. We had successfully duped 1,800 Harvard fans into holding up papers spelling out, "WE SUCK!"

Find out more about this infamous prank at HarvardSucks.org.

—*Yale University*

LESSON LEARNED: From the Yale kids, we've learned that with proper planning—and big enough balls—anything is possible. From the Harvard fans, we've learned that gullibility and intelligence are clearly not correlated.

The Few, the Proud, and the Ramen

My roommate Susan and I were outside this random party when I saw a group of guys. Being drunk, single, and consequently horny, I made my move. It took only ten minutes of conversation with one of the guys to find out: (1) he was a marine and didn't go to JMU, and (2) he was coming home with me.

So when my roommate told me she was heading to Neighbors, our local hangout, I took my new friend home. Mind you, halfway through the trip I had to ask the guy his name because I had forgotten it, but that's okay because he had forgotten mine, too. What a connection, huh?

Back at my apartment, my other roommate was giving me the "Who the hell did you bring home?" look. In my bedroom, I decided that conversation wasn't necessary, and the guy and I just went right into the hooking up. Of course, I gave him my usual "I'm not gonna have sex with you" speech, and he replied with the standard guy response, something to the effect of, "Oh, that's okay, baby. Whatever you want."

I laughed at his utter cheesiness and predictability, and then continued. About fifteen minutes into it, I heard the door slam announcing Susan's return. So I threw on my robe and went out to talk to her. I

> In 1958, the Japanese company Nissin, led by founder Momofuku Ando, introduced "Chicken Ramen," the first instant ramen.

quickly realized that all I really wanted was some ramen and some bedtime—alone, not with Mr. Marine. I returned to my room, only to find the guy on my bed wearing nothing but a pillow. When he started kissing me again, the most brilliant of plans popped into my mind.

Me: Oh shit, I have to call my friend and let her know I got in okay! (I picked up the phone and called Susan.)

> Of course I lie to people. But I lie altruistically—for our mutual good. The lie is the basic building block of good manners.
>
> —Quentin Crisp, British author

Susan: Hello?

Me: Hey, Lisa, did Mike . . . (pause for response) No way, are you serious?

Susan: Oh . . . yeah, he did.

Me: Okay, I gotta go. Later!

I turned to the guy and said, "Listen, my ex-boyfriend (hypothetical, mind you) is on his way over, and I'm still in love with him, so you have to leave!"

To his credit, the marine quickly gathered up his clothes, and the *five* condoms he had set out on my nightstand. He wished me luck with my boy, and was off into the streets of JMU at 3:00 A.M.

Then, I got my ramen and my wish to sleep in bed, alone.

—*James Madison University*

LESSON LEARNED: No situation is inescapable. In life we all have "marines"—whether it's a deadbeat friend, past baggage, or an annoying townie hookup. But with some critical thinking—and well-acted lying—you can achieve your goal . . . and savor the brothy spoils.

Laying Cable at the Russian House

Let me begin with a little background info. I had three roommates my sophomore year at Allegheny College. We shared a second-story quad in one of the older dormitories on campus. Since this dorm was ancient and had very few amenities, we were without cable or even the local TV channels. And we were without funds to pay for it.

Like any red-blooded and flat broke American, I needed to find a solution to this problem. I contacted the local cable company, who informed me that the dorm didn't have cable, and they were not willing to install it on a room-by-room basis. I called the school and got pretty much the same response. No cable was "scheduled to be installed."

That's what they thought.

Through a well-thought-out crank call, I managed to find out that our neighbor's house did indeed have cable. This house in question was only about forty feet from my second-story window, and I could see where their cable connection went into the house—two stories up, unfortunately.

This neighboring house was one of the campus-owned special-interest houses: in this case, the Russian House.

After a trip to the local Wal-Mart, we had everything we needed for my

In 2005–2006, Allegheny offered courses in ten languages, but not Russian.

plan: wire cutters, pick, track shovel, about two hundred feet of coaxial cable, a few cable splitters, white paint, and of course plenty of duct tape. I knew I could get a couple of buddies to boost me up high enough to grab the first roof, and then I could hoist the tools and myself the rest of the way up. A few more buddies would be strategically placed as lookouts.

Earlier in the day, I had waited until I saw a few of the "commies" milling around in their kitchen, and then placed a warning phone call. I introduced myself as someone from the cable company and warned them that they might be experiencing some difficulties with their cable over the next few days, until we got things ironed out. They acknowledged this, and the mission was on.

That night, I figured we'd wait until the Russians had gone to sleep to do the deed. I was dressed in black from head to toe, with a miner's light for hands-free working. We waited till about 1:00 A.M., and those damn Russians were *still* watching TV! Screw it! We went ahead with the plan anyway.

I quietly went back over to the corner of the house and started the tap in. As soon as I cut their wire I could hear one of them explaining to the others about the cable company calling and warning of difficulties. Then they all went to bed. It took me about a half hour to cut, tap in, and make it look like the wire belonged there.

Mind you, this left a new black wire running down a white house. A few of my ground men were already securing the wire to the house with some fasteners. Then, we painted the wire white to match the house. We weren't even close to being done, though. We had to bury the wire from their house to our dorm—hence the track shovel. We took turns digging a trench with a pick and shovel for the roughly forty feet from house to dorm, and then buried the wire.

We then ran the wire straight up the wall to our window and fastened it securely. Mission accomplished. We watched ESPN until about eight o'clock the next morning, dressed in black and covered in mud, and loving every minute of it.

The story does not end there. About a month later, I got to thinking how it would be great to have Cinemax, HBO, and all the good premium channels. So I made another quick call over to the Russian House. I told them I was from the cable company (again) and explained that we were running a promo to assess interest in premium channels. I also told them to call the main number to order any channels they'd like and not to worry about paying for it since it was part of this "special promo." They proceeded to order HBO, Cinemax, Playboy—the works. It was beautiful. For the last two months of the semester, we were getting all the pay-per-views and twenty-four hours of straight porn.

> According to a recent study of twenty-two regional cities in Russia, 86 percent of respondents claimed that they watched TV almost every day.

A few months ago, I ran into someone with whom I went to both high school and college. He was a few years younger, and I didn't really even know him. He came up to me at the local bar and told me he had heard all about the Russian House and us.

He said it was a legend up there. Go figure.

—*Allegheny College*

LESSON LEARNED: There's magic when it all comes together: the goal-setting, the teamwork, the ingenuity. Our author demonstrates enough positive qualities to make a career services counselor weak in the knees. Extra credit for any mission that results in twenty-four-hour porn.

Canty's Obituary Revenge

As most guys in fraternities, we were always joking around. Sometimes, though, the teasing of a brother can get to be too much. For some reason, Canty was convinced that all soccer players, like me, were fascists. He also made fun of my short soccer shorts and was known to put up pictures of Stalin in my room.

Anyway, Canty was leaving on a Thursday to go home for the weekend. We knew this and planned ahead. About five of us pooled our money (about four hundred dollars) and sent in an obituary for him to the local paper. In the write-up I described Canty as being gay and mentioned that his life partner, Gary (another guy in the house), would miss him terribly. We also noted some of his interests: watercolor painting, power walking, cooking, and furthering women's rights.

> According to Khrushchev's autobiography, Stalin frequently engaged in all-night partying with his aides, after which he would sleep all day and expect the aides to stay up and run the country.

The newspaper ran the obituary on Friday morning. The obituary stated that Canty had three cats that were going to be put to sleep if they were not adopted. We referenced his phone number for inquiries on adopting his "poor children." And with that in mind, we changed Canty's answering machine to say, "Please leave your name and number if you are interested in adopting the poor cats." We also put a banner up in front of the house that read: YOU WILL ALWAYS BE WITH US, BROTHER CANTY! For

> Death metal pioneers Obituary have released seven studio albums, including the aptly titled *Slowly We Rot* and *The End Complete*.

the final touch, one of the guys, who was an assistant editor for the daily school newspaper, slipped in a picture of Canty with the caption: "1978–2001." It was awesome.

The plan worked so well that one of the other frats canceled its party to show respect for our loss. Everyone on campus was talking about Canty's death, with great speculation over how he had died—rumors ranged from a car accident to a drug overdose. And since he was out of town, everyone bought it.

Well, Canty showed up Sunday night, and the shit hit the fan. People were freaking out as if they were seeing a ghost. Some claimed that they had never believed it, but that was a bunch of crap. Half of San Diego believed it—Canty had more messages than his machine could hold from people wanting to adopt his cats.

He took the joke pretty well, and as a bonus, he rarely called me a fascist after that.

To this day, people still say to him, "Hey, I thought you were dead."

—*San Diego State University*

LESSON LEARNED: Dream big and act quickly. Life, and college in particular, is way too short for you not to enjoy every moment of it—even if that means messing with the emotions of a community to screw with a friend.

FINAL THOUGHTS

Universities are full of knowledge; the freshmen bring a little in
and the seniors take none away, and knowledge accumulates.
—Abbott L. Lowell, Harvard president (1909–1933)

Tommy: You know, a lot of people go to college for seven years.
Richard: I know—they're called doctors.
—*Tommy Boy* (1995)

Alas, both this book and college must eventually come to an end. Class-rooms get replaced with cubicles. Empty bottles cease to be considered décor. Flip-flops and sweatpants get traded for sensible business attire. And the next thing you know, college is in the rearview mirror.

Any commencement speaker worth his fake honorary degree uses the tired cliché of graduation being the closing of one chapter and the opening of another. What they fail to mention is that the college chapter rocks. It kicks the other chapters' asses, and its dog-eared pages are proof of its popularity.

This is what attracted us to this project more than six years ago. College stories are portable, concentrated memories of this experience that people use to turn back to their favorite chapter in life.

By enjoying the nuggets in this handy collection, one sees recurring themes appear. If you hadn't already picked up on them, here are the three most important lessons:

Live in the moment. In school, you stand before a unique all-you-can-eat buffet of life. So, chow down. Suck out the marrow. Go Kobayashi on it. And don't worry about screwing up—as we've seen, embarrassment is only temporary. So savor every minute, because there's no going back (except for homecoming, but that kind of ruins our point).

Enjoy the people. Never again will you and a few hundred of your peers be packed into low-rent housing for nine months at a time. And it's too bad, because this situation creates a friendship express lane. So save your naps for class, and enjoy the 3:00 A.M. debates and fart-lighting demonstrations. Bonding like this comes around only once.

And finally, think big. If you take anything away from college life, it should be that you don't need to abide by limitations and restrictions—or sometimes even the law. Most schooling involves regurgitating facts and figures. But success in life goes to divergent thinkers—those who turn community service into a booming business or make a prank into national news.

And when thinking big fails, just listen to the sage advice of Roslyn Dominico, a University of Buffalo grad who literally bought the last word in our book on eBay.

"The most important college lesson: find an easier way. I always wanted to write a book, but never felt like writing it, so I paid other people to do it."

That's one smart grad. We couldn't be prouder.

ACKNOWLEDGMENTS

First and foremost, we'd like to recognize our readers at CollegeStories .com for letting us share your college experiences with the world. Second and just-about-foremost, we'd like to thank Christina Duffy and everyone at Random House, as well as our agent, Stephanie Kip Rostan of Levine Greenberg—without all of you this paper would be used for something much less fun. We owe a debt of gratitude to our immediate families for their support—Ben thanks Valerie, Gillian, Mel, Ed, Maggie, and Matt; Ryan thanks Vanessa, Ron, Rosemarie, Erin, and Edward Sr.; and Derrick thanks John, Shelly, Michael, and Jacquline.

Special thanks to Michael Ferrari, Cade Huninghake, and Stephanie Bennett.

Before the band starts playing to get us to hurry up, we'd like to thank the following people: Adam Herb, A. J. and Allison Rollins, Alex Blagg, Alex MacPherson, Alex Petersen, Amanda Leigh Coll, Amy Pellicane, Andre Perry, Andrej and Lexy Bajuk, Arthur Fern, Ashley Murray, Ashley Wyble, Ashlyn Broderick, Ayanna Bennett, Ben Durfey, Bob and Stacy Forchetti, Bob Whitmore, Brad and Erin Carmichael, Brad Fritz, Brad McCormick, Brendan Cassidy, Brett and Susan Balsinger, Brian and Amy Berklich, Brian Harhai, Brian and Elizabeth Whirrett, Bryan Cramer, Burt and Karen Falgui, Camille Moglia-D'Onofrio and Harry D'Onofrio, Chris Sparks, Clark Henry, Corey Hutchins, Court Sullivan, Curtis Rice, Cynthia Hope Beales Clark, Dale and Kendra Anderson, Dan Levy, Dan Stevenson, Daniel Greenberg, Dave Pava, Dave from PoopReport.com, David Aulicino, Devin J. Petroff, Don and Rachele Mock, Ed Hamilton, Elizabeth Kaletski, Ellen Gores, Emily Profeta, Eric Studer, Glenn Stevenson, Graham Verdon, Hank Lewis, Holly Dawson, Ian Asaff, Janice Lancia, Jason E. Fort, Jason Palangio, Jayce Scott, Jeff Krapels Jr., Jeff and Tracy Vanderslice, Jenn Mickler, Jenna Lux, Jim J, Jim O'Connell, Joe Ehlinger, John Cornett, John Wergeles, Joseph Fratta, J P, Keith and Annette Byran, Kembrew McLeod, Kevin Wakefield, Kirk Miller, Luther and Emily Christofoli, Mac Foster, Marc Borelli, Marc and Tasha Wisehart, Mark Lewis, Marty Lang, Mary Dalton, Mary Potts, Michael Bryan, Michael Kai, Mike Clancy, Mike and Jessica Defrank, Mike Maher, Owen Boland, Pat Cassidy, Pat Malley, Patrick and Ursula Whalen, Peter Hyman, Rich Hunt, Rob and Marci Banks, Robert Stack, Robert Wecker, Robin Muller, Ron Carpol, Ross and Leane Kuhner, Ryan Bifulco, Ryan Murphy, Sam Fasulo, Sandra Moglia, Sara Webb, Sarah Law, Scott Fullerton, Sean Gillis, Sean and Karen Stake, Shockplate, Sigma Pi Fraternity, Special Ops Media, Stephen Owens, Steve French at Creative Plumbing, Steve Grubba, Steve Hofstetter, Stiz, Tad Sterling, Ted Cotsen, Ted Johnston, Terri Pallatta, Tim Chung, Tim Duncan, Vina and Reinhold Springer, Warne and Jill Fitch, Warner May, Zach Everson.

We apologize in advance for forgetting anyone's name—our memory brain cells were killed years ago.

Left to right: Derrick, Ryan, and Ben.

BEN APPLEBAUM earned degrees in English and Communications from Wake Forest University. In 1999, he co-founded CollegeStories.com. Canadian beer drinkers know him as Slap Happy the Clown. BBQ teams know him as Judge. Originally from Pittsburgh, he is currently an advertising copywriter in Connecticut, where he lives with his wife and daughter.

RYAN MCNALLY also graduated from Wake Forest University, with degrees in English and History. His music video for metal band Shockplate earned him acclaim and hearing loss. He also created the Film Frat section of CollegeStories.com. He is the editor in chief for *Boating World* magazine and lives in Atlanta with his wife, Vanessa. View his latest video projects at your own risk at rallymcnallyproductions.com.

DERRICK PITTMAN graduated from—you guessed it— Wake Forest University with a degree in Psychology. As co-founder of CollegeStories.com, he also co-authored *Turd Ferguson & the Sausage Party: An Uncensored Guide to College Slang.* Currently, he resides in Atlanta, where he sells multipurpose game courts and putting greens.